Relax
Into
Success

A Workbook of Ancient Wisdom
for Better Living in the 21st Century

Ancient Wisdom & Modern Science

Show You How

To Have The Life

You've Always Wanted

PAUL HAIDER

Library of Congress Cataloging-In-Publication Data

Haider, Paul, 2001-
Relax Into Success—Ancient Wisdom for Better Living in the 21st Century / Paul Haider.—1st ed.

ISBN 0-9721129-0-1
Library of Congress Card Number:
2002092345

The information contained in this book is not intended to diagnose or treat any disease, condition or ailment, or serve as a replacement for professional medical or psychological advice. Any use of the information in this book is at the reader's discretion, the author and publisher specifically disclaim any and all liability arising directly or indirectly for the use or application of any information contained in this book. A health care professional should be consulted regarding your specific condition.

Much of this book has grown from my experiences doing health and wellness consultations with clients. In this book I have used slightly different situations with fictional names in order to keep all client information completely confidential.

The information contained in this book is expressed solely as the author's opinion, based on the author's research and experience.

Cover design by Natalie Beiser, Carmel, CA
Portrait photo by Rafi Claudio, San Juan, P.R.

Book design and layout by
Gloria Florit, San Juan, P.R.

In Loving Memory of Dad

About The Author

Paul Haider - Health, Prosperity & Leadership Consultant - has an extensive technical background and is very well versed in how the body works according to the allopathic model.

He has a Stress Management practice in Pacific Grove, California, helping people relax and heal using mind techniques such as hypnosis, meditation, life coaching, creative visualization, and somatic therapy. Those in combination with massage, Reiki, yoga, and fitness instruction, help people to change their habits and perceptions while learning new coping mechanisms.

Paul has worked in the field of mind/body techniques and stress management for years, and has degrees and certifications in many areas including a B.A. in Psychology (Specializing in Stress Management) and specialized certifications in Clinical Hypnotherapy, Massage, and Reiki.

He has taught technical aspects of radiology at the Universities of California (1981-1988 and 1992-1997) and Wisconsin (1988-1992). In his work, he has utilized angiograms, ultrasound, myelograms and specialized research medical techniques for more than a decade. This has given him an insightful understanding of the body.

He presented a technical research project in 1991 at the AMA Ultrasound Convention in Atlanta.

He was invited by Saunders Publishing Co. to co-write their book dealing with the technical aspects of radiology.

Paul hosted a radio show called, "Winning The Stress Wars" which aired for a long run in the Phoenix area.

His understanding of the human mind is based on his many areas of expertise and his own personal experiences. Together they provided him with a sound understanding of stress, how it works, and the benefits of stress management and balancing life.

Paul has taught meditation for years and makes it a part of his of daily ritual. He has taught one-on-one and group meditation classes, including Zen meditation, forgiveness meditations, Bhakti meditation and many other forms.

He believes in continual learning and growing, and frequently attends as well as assists personal growth groups and seminars.

Paul tells the story of a man who was a farmer in the Sacramento Valley. He raised rice and was very good at his work. He worked for a large farming company. This farmer was very proud and insisted on doing the best job he could for the company.

Sometimes in the middle of the night he would hear the wind blowing, get out of bed at 2 or 3 a.m. and sit at the kitchen table, worrying about the wind blowing the water around and knocking down the rice levees.

He started having headaches and then grinding his teeth and eventually wore his teeth down to the point he had them all extracted and had to wear dentures. During this process of wearing down his teeth, he ended up with TMJ disease and was in great pain.

The farmer worked hard and had a difficult time relaxing whenever he was not working. One spring, he had a mild heart attack, which he did not mention to anyone. In the fall of that very same year, he had a fatal heart attack and died at the age of 57. A young man struck down by stress, his life was taken long before he should have left this earth.

That man was Paul's father, and Paul misses him very much. If only his father could have learned a few techniques to eliminate stress, he might be here right now. Since then teaching people how to deal with stress has become a very important part of Paul's life. Now Paul would like to pass along what he knows, to help everyone dissolve away stress and live a happy and healthy life.

Acknowledgments

I would like to acknowledge the following people who worked to make this book possible: Jana O'Brien for her praise and caring for my work, for her love and unceasing faith in me, made the writing of this book possible; Letha Sines for all her tireless hours of editing; George Warren for doing a final edit that made the difference; Jerry Potter and Prebble for giving me encouragement and lots of helpful hints that made all the difference in the world; Bob O'Neil for his love of my writings and helping me in so many ways; Patricia Hamilton for believing in me and helping me get this book published, I owe you a lot; all of the readers of my daily e-zine column who said I should write a book; Dr. Kevin Jones for taking me under his wing and helping me to be a professional speaker. All my mentors who have helped me every step of the way: Moira Fitzgerald, Moe Ammar, Barry Dolowich, Dr. Richard Koleszar, Michael Assum, Russ Volckmann and many more, thank you for all your help; the help and support of so many friends including John Patz, Tom Burns, Merna Moyer and Greg Moleski; Natalie Bieser for her wonderful art work, I love it, Alisa Legler for her great drawings and Gloria Florit for her wonderful expertise in book design and layout, without her this book would not have materialized. To Flora Perez-Garay for more than I can put into words... you have kick started this whole project with all your wonderful love and support. I Love You. And to my family for making it all happen. Most of all to Dad, thank you for your inspiration. I wish you were here. You put the seed of creation into my mind by being who you were.

Table of Contents

Foreword

I met Paul for the first time by attending a seminar held in our conference room. When the memo came out days prior announcing the mandatory attendance of yours truly, I was thinking, "Great, just *one more thing* I have to take care of."

Looking back on it, it was the best thing that happened to me.

For the past decade I have worked in the print media field. Prior to working at the newspaper, I worked in the Information Technology department for a well-known and respected national magazine.

I know what stress is… I at times convinced myself that it was normal and I should keep marching – basically not addressing the issue. You've heard the cliches, "Deal with it", "Don't let it affect you."

How ironic, looking back upon my life juxtaposed to the new information Paul taught that serene day, that I was actually marching *backward* into a world of denial.

Was stress really worth dying for? It was time to move forward.

My personal life, at the time of my first meeting with Paul, was in shambles. A marriage gone south with the birds… a feeling of utter aninimity in a fast-paced and ever changing world. I had definitely seen better days – stress had overtaken my world… and I wasn't coping with it to the best of my abilities. I knew it. Those around me knew it. It was obvious for everyone to see.

I implore all those that come in contact with Paul to heed his advice. I, for one, had never really given Zen type of meditation and relaxation a serious thought in my life.

Perhaps you could even say I was a cynic regarding the whole thing.

Rhythmic breathing is but scratching the surface of an ocean that, with a bit of effort and a dedication of time, will cause your ship to sail calm seas. The point is not to avoid conflict, since that's foolish and denial-based, but rather to be prepared for the wicked storms that most assuredly will come your way with a refreshed, positive and willful poise to allow you to adequately temper the storm, and allow you, the sailor, to continue your journey through life with more knowledge and appreciation about and
for yourself.

Of this, I know. Paul will teach you, too.

Ash Fox
Manager, Information Technology
Newspaper Columnist

Introduction

Life is about balance, when an area of life gets out of balance it creates stress. It is important to find out what is holding you back from having a balanced life. A balanced life increases health, well-being, happiness, creativity, productivity, wealth, and peace of mind. In the following chapters you will find out what's holding you back from balancing your life, and what to do to achieve the life you've always wanted.

Learning how to deal with stress is a necessity in our daily lives. We need to be armed with the right tools. Stress has the ability to lower our immune system, allowing disease to step in. At one time the only stress we had was just trying to stay alive by running away from a hungry lion or some other wild beast. In our process of running away, we let go of all the pent-up stress. Nowadays we have a hard time running away from the wild beast that chases us. Today the wild beast is our boss or the corporation or the government or any other institution, situation or dogma that seems to have hold power over us.

The proper way to handle stress is to do it in a positive way. To surmount stress is to make changes and to confront the problems instead of just letting them all build up to the point where stress is killing you. Stress will not go away on its own; steps have to be taken to make changes in life in order to have stress disappear.

Every day we are bombarded by all kinds of stress, from heavy traffic to a death in the family, divorce, poor health, etc. Sometimes we are caught between two undesirable alternatives and have to choose the lesser of two evils.

Eastern medicine is becoming very popular as an adjunct to western medicine in our society. It is very important to take the best of both worlds and integrate both types of thought. In this book I will address many different types of stress-reducing techniques, each of value to the average person. I will also be addressing life balancing as another area that helps to eliminate stress from a person's life. Life balancing is taking the six key elements of life—mind, body, spirit, relationships, social interactions, and financial aspects of life—and making sure all are in balance with one another. These six major areas of life are supported by our core beliefs. Be it a belief in science, a Creator, God or whatever, this core of beliefs is like glue, holding the major elements of our life together.

If everyone took the time to relax and let go of our worries, we would be much more at peace and be more creative, thus accomplishing more throughout our workday.

According to Willis (1988), doctors say 80 to 85% of all illnesses they see are directly related to stress.

Dr. Herbert Benson (1997) talks about an average of 75% of all doctor visits being related to stress. There are 670,000 physicians in this country and each has on the average 72.4 patients per week or a total of 3,858.4 office visits per doctor per year. The average cost per visit is $56.20 each. If you take the number of doctors times their number of patient visits, times the cost per visit, this comes to a total of 145.3 billion dollars a year on health care! Benson estimates at least half of the 75% caused by stress could be eliminated with a little home health. In the end this translates to 54.3 billon dollars a year that can be saved on health care just by teaching people how to relax and let go of stress (Benson, 1997). Job stress is estimated to cost U.S. industry $300 billion annually, as assessed by absenteeism, diminished productivity, employee turnover, and direct legal and insurance fees.

This doesn't even take into account medical procedures, over the counter medications, prescriptions, or days away from work. So you can see, just in dollars it makes a lot of sense to eliminate stress, and it is very relevant to helping our society change for the better.

I know from my own personal experience that if I am relaxed I am happier, and if I am happy, my feelings of being happy seem to rub off on everyone around me. So I truly feel if we lower our stress levels, we will be a happier, healthier, society.

Stress is a very serious problem, and it is getting worse all the time. Every time we have a death in the family, a major change in our living conditions, divorce, children leaving home, marriage, business changes, retirement, responsibility changes at home or work, violations of law, change in health, moving home, loss of job, pregnancy, changing schools, beginning or stopping school, trouble with relatives, all these things and more increase the amount and severity of stress in our lives.

In this fast-paced world we live in we are bombarded with more stress than ever because we move more frequently, we have more to remember, we have to achieve more education than ever before. In the past we were born, lived and died all in the same town. We knew just what we were going to do for a living, because the family business would become ours in the future. We might move once or twice in a lifetime, but that was it. Now we move much more often.

A small amount of stress keeps us moving and changing, motivated, and wanting to deal with life. But large amounts of stress, or constant small amounts of stress, can destroy our lives, causing us to fall prey to disease and perhaps death. Stress also has side effects on relationships, friends and relatives.

Whenever we have fearful or negative thoughts, our bodies are filled with a chemical called cortisol. Cortisol is a very powerful chemical, which lowers our immune system there by opening the door to disease. So we are creating something out of nothing. From thoughts, we create matter in the form of a chemical that wreaks havoc over our bodies, and eventually if not controlled, our lives (Benson, 1998).

What is Success?

Success means many things to many people. Some people think success is having lots of money. For others success is having a wonderful relationship. And still for others it's having a great body. There are as many different ideas about what success is… as there are people.

But most of us have never given any thought to what success means to us. So take the time now to think about what success means to you and write your answer down below.

- _____

- _____

- _____

- _____

Now if you achieve what you wanted above, and end up having health problems because you didn't take care of your body. Is that success? Or, if you have a great body but neglect your finances and end up destitute. Is that success? When you really get down to it, life at its best is balancing all parts of your life.

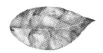

Balance

1. **Do you find yourself feeling that life should have more to offer?**
2. **Is your mind, body, spirit, social, and financial life out of kilter?**
3. **Do you feel one aspect of your life is not working?**
4. **Do you need direction?**
5. **Are you working harder and enjoying it less?**
6. **Are you ready for a life changing plan?**

Nowadays we have so much going on. We need a break just as much as we need to get things done. Balancing life is something we take for granted. *"Of course my life is balanced, I'm alive aren't I?"* That's usually the way we think about taking time to look at our lives from a different perspective.

Technology has allowed us to do more in less time. By itself that's great; but no one has taken into consideration that the human mind, body and spirit can do only so much. Technology was intended to save us from work, but in reality has done just the opposite, allowing us to get so much done that we just keep doing and doing. So technology has loaded us with more than the average person can handle. This does not mean technology is bad; on the contrary, it is wonderful, but we have to learn to balance it with the rest of our life.

It is possible to achieve this balance of mind, body, spirit, relationships, social aspects & financially. And it can be accomplished simply.

Just think of a six-pointed star. Along each line starting from the center of the star, number from one to ten, with ten being an aspect of your life which is well rounded, and one being an aspect which is lacking in some way. The following chart depicts this image.

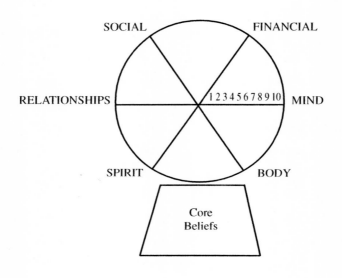

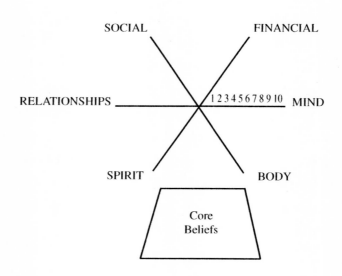

Place a dot along the line of the star at points coinciding with where you feel you are in each area of life balancing. Now draw around the outside of the star connecting the dots. Each dot should connect with the next to create a nice round circle or wheel that rolls along instead of having to be pushed or pulled through life.

Another way to think about having a balanced life is to think of each area of your life as dominos all standing perfectly straight on end, all six aligned one after the other. If one or more of the areas of life, or dominos, gets out of balance and tips over there is a cascade effect knocking down all the rest of the dominos.

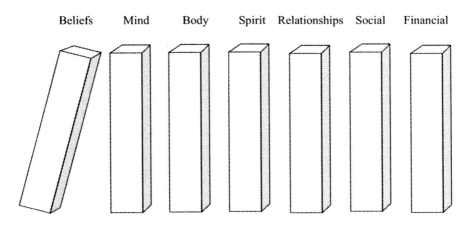

The Dominos of Life—They Could All Fall Down

A well rounded, balanced life will roll easily and each area will stand tall like a pillar. An unbalanced life will not roll and all areas will end up falling over in the end, for each area depends on the other for stability and the ability to hold life together.

The Mind

A university professor went to visit a famous Zen master.
While the master quietly served tea, the professor talked about Zen.
The master poured the visitor's cup to the brim, and then kept pouring.
The professor watched the overflowing cup
until he could no longer restrain himself.

"It's overfull!
No more will go in!" the professor blurted.
"You are like this cup," the master replied,
"How can I show you Zen unless you first empty your cup"

—Zen Story

1. **Are you a lifelong-learner?**
2. **Do you take time to read everyday?**
3. **Are you a positive thinker?**
4. **Do you have lifelong goals?**
6. **Do you express your emotions, or hold them in?**
7. **Do you live life in the future or in the past?**

In this day and age we have so much going on in our lives we sometimes get overwhelmed. I liken our minds to a computer. Have you ever opened an application on your PC, and then another, and then another, and another, and all of a sudden the mouse quits moving, then you have to reboot and start over?

This is what happens to our mind. We have all kinds of things going on, such as thinking we have to take the kids to school, go to work, go to the bank, go shopping, pick things up at the cleaners, call the plumber, take the kids to scouts, make dinner, call and make reservations for the weekend and on and on and on until all of a sudden we feel overwhelmed and stop moving. Just like the computer we need a break, we need time to just be, time to let go and not think.

I find it interesting that so many great speakers, successful business people, and therapists recommend taking thirty minutes a day to just be in silence. Take time to clear your jumbled thoughts and let go of those frantic feelings. Yes, I said frantic—that feeling you get when you have so many things to do and don't know which one to work on first. The feeling that everything needs your attention right now. The truth of the matter is that only a couple of those things really need your attention now, and the others will wait. Being frantic doesn't accomplish anything. When we take the time to be silent we emerge able to accomplish more than we ever thought possible.

Try it

Make sure the telephone is off or in the silent mode. Tell everyone you are going to take a few minutes for yourself, sit down, relax and get comfortable. Take a couple of good long breaths and key in on your breathing. That's right, concentrate on your breath, in and out, just imagining your breath coming in from the tip of your nose to the bottom of your lungs, and from the bottom of your lungs to the tip of your nose, in and out, in and out—you're doing great. Now if a thought comes in just say, *"I see that, but not right now,"* and go back to concentrating on your breathing. Breathe from the tip of your nose to the bottom of your lungs, and from the bottom of your lungs to the tip of your nose. Remember, whenever a thought comes to mind don't try to push it out, just say to yourself, *"I see that, but not right now,"* and go back to concentrating on your breathing. Just keep this up and eventually you'll notice that time flies by—but it does take some practice.

Letting go of thoughts takes practice. Welcome to the practice of meditation! That's right, I said meditation. It is easy and you don't have to sit in the lotus position or do anything esoteric, it is just letting go of thoughts.

Be Happy

We're so used to thinking all the time that we have a hard time just being. You know that old saying "Be Happy?" It's not "Do Happy." We get so caught up in this world of thinking and doing to the point that we don't have any time to just *be*.

Just think about tribes of people back through antiquity. They got up in the morning, perhaps made love, enjoyed everyone's company, completed their rituals and finally went off to hunt and gather food for three or four hours. Upon their return they enjoyed the company of the whole tribe, interacting with everyone and enjoying a lazy afternoon. They would talk and tell stories, eat dinner, and fall off to sleep. Yes, there was time for doing things, but nothing like today.

Do you think they had problems falling asleep at night or relaxing? No! I don't think so. They did have their stressors, like wild animals and drought. But for the most part, life was slow going and they had a lot of down time.

Our bodies and minds have not progressed far from that point in time, we still need down time, and we still need time to be. So take a hint from successful people and take a few minutes to just be in the silence. Your day will flow so much better.

In addition I find at the end of my meditation that wonderful creative thoughts come to me—thoughts I would never have had if I hadn't taken the time to let go of thinking. When we have a little bit of down time our thinking is rejuvenated, and we find all kinds of answers to problems we couldn't answer before. If you want to be creative, try being silent for awhile.

Keep Learning

Do you know anyone who has stopped learning and says they've learned enough in their lifetime? I knew just such a person. He was blind and deaf and had a hard time getting around. He was also very angry that all this had happened to him so he decided to cut off his nose to spite his face, so to speak. He sat around all day doing nothing, being alone and then going to bed and sleeping a lot, and ended up being depressed. It was so sad because this person was a teacher, and could have been teaching people Math, making a difference in other's lives, but he decided to give up and basically die.

Interestingly enough, without any stimulation this person started to see things and hear things that weren't there, and to have crazy dreams. If the mind isn't stimulated it starts stimulating itself, causing all kinds of hallucinations. So you see, we need to keep learning and stimulating our minds or it will do it for us!

I learn something new every day even if I don't want to, for if I am up and around I will learn something new just because I'm going through the process of living.

The mind is a growing organ that needs stimulation. It needs nutrition just like our bodies. Keep it fueled well, keep it growing or it will do its own thing, as this person found out.

My own mother tried to say she didn't need to know anything else and locked herself away in the house. But after awhile she started going stir-crazy and needed stimulation so she signed up for computer classes. I was floored! Then flower arranging classes and so forth, and now she just keeps learning day after day. Now she's making life happen.

Life is the process of learning. When we give up learning, we give up life, so keep moving forward allowing your *self* to change, grow and learn.

Are you learning on a constant basis?

• _____*Yes,* _____*No*

If not, what could you do to keep learning?

- _____

- _____

- _____

The Big Six Goals

We all need something to strive for, something that keeps us motivated, something that keeps us attuned to life and loving life. We all need goals! We need to keep pushing our limits! Oh, I know what you're saying, "You just told us we need down time, time to be, and that seems incongruent with striving." But you know what? We can do both, we can have our time to be, and we can stay busy. There is nothing wrong with being busy. If we're not, our mind will create stimulation like that woman I just talked about. So move forward and make plans, make plans for tomorrow, next week, next month, next year, five years down the road, and for life.

List six goals you want to accomplish in your lifetime. Six things that are really important to you! You know, like getting through school, or getting married, or taking that wonderful vacation to the islands. Whatever they are, write them down, make an intention, and put it out to the Universe.

Make a list of goals you want to accomplish

- _____

- _____

- _____

- _____

- _____

- _____

Use additional sheets of paper and make a list of 50 goals for your life.

You may want to have two or three lists of goals, one for personal goals like losing weight, another for the office like making the projected sales, and yet another for life goals you want to accomplish while you're on this planet. Make these lists and keep them with you all the time. Make a card you can put in your purse or billfold, and look at it often.

You say that is all well and good, but just looking at this list won't make it happen. You're right! But by looking at your list and thinking about it you can create your dreams. Maybe you think you can't create something from nothing. Whenever we have a thought, we create chemicals in our brains that rush throughout our bodies relaying our emotional state or feelings. So we can create something from nothing. It is from this nothingness that we create all of life. If only we believe we can do it, and strive to make it happen every day, eventually it will happen. If you let go of your goals and forget about them, nothing will ever happen. But if you look at them all the time and make plans, working toward those goals, then your goals will be a reality.

Do you want a new house? Then say to yourself that your goal is to have a new house and start saving for that house. Did you know if you started saving $10 a day, over thirty years you would accumulate a million dollars? All it takes is an intention and working toward your goal. No, this is not magic; it is just putting mind together with daily routine to make things happen. It is a lot different from wishful thinking. Just hoping you'll have a house someday will never make it happen. With intentions you make it happen with action to back it up.

Sometimes intentions leave you open to the possibility that something will happen. Then when the right opportunity comes along you will be ready to take action and make your move.

Once I wanted to move to Monterey, CA from the Sacramento area. At that time I didn't see any way of doing this. I was working at a job I'd had for over ten years and didn't see a way to leave. But out of the blue a person came into my life and asked me where I wanted to live. I said Monterey. We moved there and started a business. If I didn't have that intention to move, I never would have picked up on the fact that this was an open opportunity. It would have never happened. So make intentions, make plans, keep an open mind, and look for open doors. It will all work out if you really want it to.

What would you like to see happen in your life?

- _____

- _____

- _____

Create a Time Line

Now create a time line. Make a calendar of events you want to happen in your life. Write your goals on your calendar and put down set times to be at certain places in your life. Include your vacations, your dreams, and your family life. Everything should be taken into account. Check up on yourself on a regular basis. Refer back to this calendar every week, and make plans for the next week to make dreams come true. This calendar should be large because some of your dreams will need time to happen. Create a calendar that spans 10 years. Check on your progress and make adjustments accordingly.

Now make your Goals calendar on a separate piece of paper. If this is difficult, what holds you back from creating your dreams?

- _____

- _____

- _____

- _____

Use the Buddy System

Once you have set goals you need someone to help you achieve them. Find someone you can buddy with to help each other achieve your end results. Break down your goals into yearly, quarterly, monthly, and weekly segments as part of your working game plan.

Set up weekly meetings to talk over what you want to achieve toward your goals. Many of us make plans, set goals, but never implement them. Putting our plan into action takes moving out of our comfort zone. This is where the buddy system really works. Two people giving support and checking on the progress of each other makes it so much easier to move past barriers which keep you from moving forward toward your goals. We all procrastinate, but when we have someone coaching us it makes getting things done so much easier.

Who are you going to ask to be your buddy?

- _____

When is your first weekly meeting?

- _____

Find Some Mentors

You can't do it all by yourself, so find some people you look up to who are willing to help you attain your goals. Find people you feel are successful and ask them to be your mentor. You will be surprised just how flattered people are when you ask them if you might call them for advice once in a while. Most people will be glad to help in any way they can. If they don't have the time or energy, ask someone else. Remember they are where you want to be, and they have learned many lessons along the way which they can pass on to you. I have eight wonderful mentors in my life that have helped me immensely.

Who are you going to ask to be your mentor? List at least four people you would like to have as your mentor.

- _____

- _____

- _____

- _____

Group of Like-Minded Positive Thinking People

Put together a group of like-minded, positive thinking people, people who are interested in moving towards a better life. Find people you enjoy being around, have something in common with, and have something to share with the group. Use this group to share thoughts, think things over, and generally support one another with ideas, moral support, and connections. These people are different from your mentors. This group of people are people like you, wanting to move forward in life.

The power of one positive thinking person is amazing, the power of many positive thinking people is astounding. Meet once a month so you can help each other move toward your goals.

Who are you going to invite to be a part of your like-minded positive thinking group?

- _____

When is your first meeting scheduled?

- _____

Optimism

One of the major things researchers have found with centenarians, people who have lived for over 100 years, is a spirit of optimism, a spirit of never giving up (Winter, 1999; Kimmel, 1990). If you keep trying, the odds are in your favor, sooner or later you're going to roll the dice and win. It is a 50-50 proposition, no matter what we do, we can win or lose, but in the long run if we keep trying sooner or later we will win.

Are you an optimist?

- _____ *Yes,* _____ *No*

If not, from whom did you learn to be negative?

- _____

- _____

- _____

Believe in Yourself

In order to win we have to believe in ourselves, and this can be hard if you were told as a kid you could never do anything right. Those old tape loops play over and over telling you that you are a loser. They have to be looked at and understood for what they are—lies! Once you identify them and find out where they came from, you can allow them to disappear and make new positive tape loops to take their place.

Take a look in the mirror and say to yourself, *"I can do anything I really want to do."* Look in your eyes, look down deep and feel what's coming up for you as you look at yourself in the mirror. When a reaction to what you just said comes up, say it out loud. Perhaps you're saying, *"I can do anything"* and then all of a sudden, in the back of your mind you hear the words, *"No I can't, there's no way, I'm not that smart."* Then rebut what you just heard and say, *"Oh yes I can, I am as intelligent as anyone else on this planet."* Say this out loud and look at yourself. It is time for you to get this all straightened out and start moving forward in life. Then listen again and note what that little voice is saying, *"Oh no I can't,*

I'm afraid," and answer back out loud, *"Yes I'm afraid, but lots of great people have been afraid and have done great things anyway."* And keep doing this until that little voice in the back of your mind stops saying all those negative things. This is coaching you, from you, and for you, and the best type of therapy there is, so do it every day until that little nagging voice turns into a positive reassuring voice, saying things like *"You can do it, I know you can."*

What does your little nagging voice tell you?

- _____

- _____

Now write down positive answers to the nagging voice.

- _____

- _____

- _____

- _____

Having taken care of the nagging voice, write down a *positive affirmation for yourself that will help you through life. Keep it short and always in a positive tone. Don't include the words "no", "won't", "should", "will". Use the words "I AM."*

- *I am*

  _____

- *I am*

  _____

The Mind Creates Non-Reality

Think about that little nagging voice. The fact of the matter is that 97% of the time most things we worry about never happen, and 2% of the time they happen just slightly the way we worried about and only 1% of the time does it actually happen the way we worried it might happen. So what are you worrying about in the first place? We do all that worrying for that 1%. Well, that seems like a waste of time to me. Perhaps it would be better to think about how 97 % of the time everything works out the way we wanted. Our mind creates terrible scenarios of what might happen and we dwell on that 1% all the time. Just think about it, does that seem ridiculous or what? We spend all that time worrying about something a bookie wouldn't bet on. Start betting on the winning part of life and stop all that worrying for nothing.

Sometimes our mind also creates non-realities by creating a story that we are part of, and then all of a sudden we forget we made up the story. Have you ever fallen in love with someone overnight? Created this amazing story about this life and this person and then got lost in the story? The mind is a master at making up stories and forgetting to tell you that you're part of a story. Once we click in with the story we are lost. We become part of the professional actors on stage performing this dramatic scene from the best screenwriters I know— "Ourselves."

So remember you're the storyteller and don't get lost in the play. Do a reality check, pinch yourself, is this real or did I just make this up? If you decide you made it up, then you have a chance to step out of the part you're playing and end the scene. But you might also decide it is not real and decide to play the part anyway, and that's O.K., as long as you know the truth. Just play your part with all your heart, for this is your life.

Have you written any stories in your mind about yourself that are non-reality based?

- _____

Write down what the truth of this story really is.

- _____

- _____

The Mind Needs To Be Watched

If we allow our mind to do whatever it wants, it takes over and runs amuck, allowing all kind of thoughts to take root. We have to make sure we spend time on a regular basis watching what we think about.

There is a story of a man who is given a gift of a robot (the mind) from Master saying, "This robot can do anything you want it to do. It can wash your car, do the laundry, take care of the children, make the bed, do the dishes; whatever you want, this robot (mind) can do it."

"Sounds great," said the man, so he had the robot doing everything, even paying his bills. It got to the point he didn't really have to do anything, the robot did it all.

After a few days he became bored and decided to go down to the local bar and have a drink. He ended up so soused he barely made his way home.

To his horror, upon opening the door he gazed upon an unbelievable site. The robot had stacked all the furniture in the middle of the living room, had set it ablaze and was roasting two of the neighbor's children over the fire.

This is a dramatic teaching story, which shows how our mind can get carried away, making up some of the most absurd ideas and ways of dealing with life when we don't think about what we are thinking.

When a thought comes into your head, check it. Is this the kind of representative "thought" you would like to have? If not, replace that thought with something positive.

Themes

Have you noticed that themes seem to replay themselves in your life? Do you understand that they will keep looping back around as long as it takes you to learn something from them? Once you have learned a lesson and valued from it, you move past it as long as you use what you have learned to make a difference in your life.

Life is like a spiral of time we travel along. On our journey along this spiral, there will be themes that appear here and there. They are not exactly the same time and space being revisited again, but we are revisiting again what we haven't learned. Like old photos and old memories, these themes are very hard to throw away. They are familiar, comfortable, and we only have the courage to throw them away when we finally learn the lesson. Then that theme is ejected from the spiral of life and we travel down the road ready to meet the next challenging theme.

Write down a list of life themes that seem to reappear in your life. Next write down ways of dealing with these recurring life themes. For instance, if you're unlucky in love, perhaps it is time for you to love yourself. If you find it hard to have peace with your brother, then perhaps it's time to make peace with yourself. For every question there is an answer. We just have to open our eyes to all the possibilities.

- _____

- _____

- _____

Fear

Many people feel there are only two ways of being in this life. We can either come from a place of fear or from a place of love. You may say that's not true. What about anger, depression, blame, joy, excitement, ecstasy, and more? If we look deep at all these feelings, they either come from Love or Fear. Anger stems from not feeling in control, or the fear of not being in control. Joy develops from a place of self-love, for we don't have any joy in our life without allowing ourselves to have joy. So it is joy that allows us to feel joyous. So, as you can see, it does all boil down to Love or Fear.

What do you want for your life? Do you want your life to be ruled by Fear? Or do you want your life to be ruled by Love?

Fear can be a great motivator, but is that the way you want to live your life...always in fear of something happening, always in fear of others, always in fear of the next bend in the river of life? Oh, fear will get you up and moving all right, but in the end fear doesn't create any positive changes in life. Fear chooses to rule life from behind the eight ball, by taking care of the brush fires of life, instead of being on top of the eight ball and ahead of the game, making plans for the future. Fear motivates by *having* to do, Love motivates by *wanting* to do.

Every challenge we face is rooted in fear. From wars to marital strife, to problems in government, fear drives the need to protect ourselves all the time.

The next thing that happens to redirect us from loving, is the fear of stepping out of our comfort zone. When we start loving ourselves, it doesn't feel comfortable so we automatically step back into fear saying, "*No I can't do that, it doesn't feel comfortable,*" and we are once again driven by fear.

Make changes in yourself, be loving to yourself and everyone around you, and then stick with it. You can live your life from a place of love. I didn't say it would be easy! On the contrary, it will be hard! But by all means it will extend and make your life much more joyful.

Are you fear driven or love driven? Do you have to be forced to do things? Fear driven. Or are you always extending yourself trying to make life better for yourself and everyone around you before anything happens? Love driven.

Answer these questions to find out which one you are.

Do you pay your bills on time?

• _____

If so, do you pay then because you want to or have to?

• _____

Do you ever take time for yourself?

• _____

Do you make it a point to be on time?

• _____

Because you don't want to be late or because it is easier on you?

• _____

Do you eat healthy food?

● _____

Because you are afraid of the consequences of not eating healthy?

● _____

Or because you feel better when you eat right?

● _____

When you're on vacation do you enjoy the time off?

● _____

Or are you just itching to get back to the office?

● _____

What do you need to do to start loving yourself and working from a place of love instead of fear?

● _____

● _____

● _____

Anger

Anger can be the enemy and at the same time it can be a wonderful tool. When your life is threatened and you need to protect yourself, anger is a wonderful emotion that comes to your rescue to keep you and your loved ones alive.

At the same time out-of-control anger can be ugly, causing all sorts of rash decisions that may even end up hurting someone. Anger keeps our mind out of touch with our creative abilities, our intuition, and our innate ability to know what's right. Anger boils with rage, and if held in it has a deleterious effect on our bodies.

I know of a woman who worked with women who had been put in prison unjustly. She dealt with the legal system by trying to help these women get out from behind bars. This whole process was a struggle. She felt so much anger that she started to live her life just to help these women. She wouldn't let go of the anger, and a year later was diagnosed with cancer. Also in a recent study, angry young people were noted to have an increase in heart attacks.

What are you angry about, or with whom are you angry? Take the time now to list anything you are angry about.

- _____

- _____

- _____

Depression

Depression can stem from many different causes. One of the major causes is anger held within. In this society we are told not to show our anger, "Don't get angry with me, little mister, or I'll give you something to be angry about." We don't know how to express our anger in a positive way. We think anger is a negative emotion.

I've seen many people holding in so much anger that it expresses itself as sadness. It is like having a huge iron pot in the middle of your chest. You put your anger in the pot and keep adding more and more. Soon you have to sit on the lid to keep it closed. Once in a while, so much anger builds up inside that the lid pops open. Anger bursts forth like hot steam hurting everyone around at the time instead of the people with whom you are really angry. It is usually the people you love who end up hurting instead of the people you are really angry with.

You need to release your anger and let it out in a positive way. Here is a list of a few positive ways to release anger:

1. Find a secluded place to yell and scream. Perhaps scream in your car in the middle of the night. You might try screaming into a pillow in your bedroom when no one is around.

2. If you have a trusted friend who might help, have him/her hold you from behind around your abdomen. Scream from deep down in your abdomen, way down in the middle of your guts. Having someone you love hold you allows you to feel safe and helps you to let it all out. They might even scream along with you, helping you to release your anger. Of course you need a room or secluded place to do this. I've done this many times at workshops and have even seen 80-year-old people use this technique with great success.

3.   For me, if I'm doing some anger work and walking into the bedroom and hitting the bed with a plastic bat until I can do it no longer works great. Then I finally break down and cry, releasing all of my pent-up emotion.

4.   Another way that works for some people is to journal. Write out every single thing you are angry about. It is cathartic to write it all down. It is as though all that anger is being transferred to the written page and given up to the Universe to resolve.

5.   You can write down a list of things you are angry about, then set it on fire. Make a ritual of it, letting go of all the stuff smoldering within you.

6.   Exercise can be a wonderful way of letting go of anger. Feel the anger as you exercise, push that weight while you think about being angry, run has hard as you can while feeling your anger. Play tennis and swing every swing with anger and let it all out, get it all worked out to the point you're dead tired. Do this with the purpose of releasing your anger; don't do it for just the purpose of exercising. Make it a point to do it with your anger in mind.

7.   Most important of all, when you are angry take a time out by saying, "I'm angry." I'm going to do some anger release work, and I'll be back." Then come back and confront the problem when you've cooled off. Don't deal with the problem while you're still angry.

How are you going to deal with your anger?

- _____

- _____

Forgiveness

After you have released your anger, the key to keep it from coming back is forgiveness! You're forever locked in battle with this overwhelming feeling called anger if you don't allow yourself to forgive and move on with life. Forgiveness is not for the other person, it is for you! Anger eats away at your body and soul. Do yourself a favor and allow yourself to forgive so you can start living life.

For some of us, forgiving someone for something horrendous they have done to us is not easy. How do you forgive someone for rape or murder? Sometimes it helps to imagine yourself stepping into their body, and feeling what torment they must be going through... the numbness, the hatred, feel it all. Now, having felt what's going on inside of them, check on what you are feeling. Most of the time we feel very sad about such a tormented soul. Now take this sadness and allow it to help you to forgive.

Many times the most important person to forgive is ourself for what we feel we have done to hurt someone else. This feeling of having done something hurtful holds us back from ever developing into the truly wonderful person we are. We can never have the life we want if we constantly feel we have wronged others. After it's all said and done there is nothing more we can do but forgive ourselves for our own mistakes.

List all the people in this world you need to forgive including yourself and why.

- _____

- _____

- _____

- _____

Blaming

Have you ever noticed people who tend to blame everyone for their problems? They tend to think everyone else is to blame for all their problems, the whole world is against them, and they have nothing to do with making life work. Do you ever see these people getting anywhere in life? Of course not, they are stuck doing the same thing over and over again, blaming everyone. "They're against me. It's all their fault. I can't get ahead if they keep doing *that* to me." These are some of the phrases people who blame tend to use.

But you know what? There are no "theys." There is only "me." The only one to blame for my problems is myself for not dealing with them. Blame doesn't change anything, it only keeps us stuck in the past. The past is over and done with and will never come around again.

Who have you been blaming for your problems? Be honest and make a list, including yourself, and for what.

- _____

- _____

- _____

Say to yourself, "I am the maker of my life," releasing anyone from blame from this time forward. *"From here on out, I alone create my life."*

Live in the Here-and-Now

If you're blaming, you are stuck in the past and the past is already done. You can never go back and redo the past. As long as you hold onto it, the past will keep recreating itself. If you hold on to the past with such tenacity that it seems like today, then your life today is already decided for you. You will relive the past for as long as you hold onto it.

Living Life
We search yet we do not see
We see yet we will not touch
We know yet we will not understand
Releasing the past
we finally see
take hold
and understand.——————— Paul Haider, ©, 1999

The future has not yet arrived and living in the future doesn't bring satisfaction in life. Only living at this very moment brings any kind of satisfaction. The future has many different possibilities and opportunities. We don't know what possibilities will happen. But if we constantly live for tomorrow, trying to make the future what we think it should be, we have totally lost the joy of this very moment. Because, we are lost in the future. Do what you can do right now and leave the future for the future. It will come soon enough. Don't be impatient because in doing so you will suddenly wake up and wonder what happened to the years, all those years you lost planning and doing solely for the future. This is a piece I truly love. I think it sums it up very nicely:

The Station

Tucked away in our subconscious is an idyllic vision. We see ourselves on a long trip that spans the continent. We are traveling by train. Looking out the windows we drink in the passing scene of cars on nearby highways, of children waving at a crossing, of cattle grazing on a distant hillside, of smoke pouring from the power plant, of row upon row of corn and wheat, of flat land and valleys, of mountains and rolling hillsides, of city skylines and village halls.

But uppermost in our mind is the final destination. Bands will be playing and flags waving. Once we get there our dreams will come true and pieces of our lives will fit together like a jigsaw puzzle. How restlessly we pace the aisles, damning the minutes for loitering—waiting, waiting, waiting at the station.

"When we reach the station, that will be it!" we cry.

"When I'm 18."

"When I buy a new Mercedes."

"When I put the last kid through college."

"When I have paid off the mortgage!"

" When I get a promotion."

"When I reach the age of retirement, I shall live happily
ever after!"

Sooner or later we must realize there is no station, no one place at which to arrive, once and for all. The true joy of life is the journey. The station is only a dream. It constantly outdistances us.

Regret and fear are twin thieves that rob us of today. So stop pacing the aisles and counting the miles. Instead climb more mountains, eat more ice cream, go barefoot more often, swim more rivers, watch more sunsets, laugh more, and cry less. Life must be lived as we go along. The station will come through soon enough.
—*Author Unknown.*

What are you waiting for? Is it the past that holds you back from living this very moment? Or is it worry about the future that keeps you from being fully alive?

Make a list of things that hold you in the past, and then a list of worries about the future that keep you locked into the future.

The Past

● _____

● _____

The Future

- _____

- _____

Now look at all these items you have listed and make a list of why you should let go of them. Why should you let go of the past? Why should you let go of the worries of the future?

- _____

- _____

- _____

There is a Zen story about a man who was running away from a tiger, who fell over a cliff and was able to grab the root of a small plant. Tiger above him, sharp rocks below, and the root giving way. Being in the moment he saw a nice strawberry plant growing within arm's reach. He plucks a nice fat strawberry, and forgetting the past, the tiger, and the future, death on the rocks below, he tastes the strawberry. "What a nice strawberry," he says. This story depicts what being in the Moment or in the Here-and-Now is all about.

Now write down both lists on another piece of paper and place them in the fireplace and set them on fire. Watch as the pieces of paper curl and turn black and become nothing more than ashes. At this same time say to yourself, "I now release the past and the future, living my life in the here-and-now from this point on."

Goals are future-oriented of course, but it is doing what you can do right now that counts and not worrying about what life might bring that offers fulfillment.

Discipline: Connect with Passion

Changing your lifestyle has nothing to do with how much money you earn, what you look like, where you live, or anything like that; it all has to do with discipline. Like losing weight, are you ready to put in the time and be relentless in your pursuit? What is your passion? Only passion will drive you toward your goal! Can you link what you desire with your passion? What is so fulfilling to you that you would do it for free?

Now take your desire, link it with your passion and you can accomplish anything!

List your passions. Write down what you truly enjoy in life.

- _____

- _____

- _____

Now use this list of passions to link them with your goals in life, and make life happen!

Short-Term Personal Goals

Once you have released the past and the future, you need to work on the present. What can you do today to make your life better? What does your life need right now that will make a difference today?

Write down your list of short-term goals. Use additional paper if necessary.

- _____

- _____

- _____

These goals might be as simple as a new job or as complex as choosing a new direction in life. What little thing can you do that will start you on your way? Is there a magazine that will give you ideas or point you in the right direction? What about going to the library and looking up information on what you really want in your life? The Internet also has all kinds of information. Try looking there.

Now write down twelve things you can do this month that will make a difference in your life.

- _____

- _____

- _____

- _____
- _____
- _____
- _____
- _____
- _____
- _____
- _____
- _____

Write these twelve items on your calendar.

Make a promise to yourself to keep your schedule and always move forward to the next challenge. Then move on to the next month and the month after that, until all of a sudden you have accomplished what you wanted. You can do this! Just take one item at a time on your calendar and go for it!

Life Goals

What six goals did you write down that you want to accomplish in your lifetime?

I happen to know someone who had a list of 120 things he wanted to accomplish in his lifetime, and at the age of 39 he was on item 83. Not bad! So, what about you? Six things to accomplish are nothing compared to 120, so you can do it too! Before you die, what would you like to do? What would really make your soul sing? Don't say, "Oh, it's not possible" and dismiss your dreams just like that!

Now write down six more life goals.

1._____

2._____

3._____

4._____

5._____

6._____

This list can expand at any time; just keep it and add to it on a regular basis. These goals don't have to make sense to anyone else. Perhaps you have always wanted to go to Paris, France ever since you were a little kid. Anything and everything is a worthy goal! Anything you can think of is worthwhile; don't let the thoughts of others get in your way. It is *your* life. Live your life the way *you* want!

People who are about to die say the same things:
1. I wish I had taken more risks!
2. I wish I had had more relationships in my life!
3. I wish I had played hooky from the office more often!
4. I wish I had taken better care of myself!
5. I wish I had done something more fulfilling with my life!
6. I wish!

Don't make wishes or dream about how life should be! Make your life be true to your wishes! Then you won't have any regrets at the end of your life.

Go back to your calendar and write down your list of life goals. Write them down for the next ten years and beyond. Now make yourself reminders as to what you need to do to prepare to make your goals come true.

Write down a sequence of events that need to happen to make that goal come true. Then write down that sequence of events on your calendar in a realistic fashion. **Example:** If you want to sail the world, first you need to take sailing classes. Start with novice sailing one month and work up to bareboat classes in a few months. Then go on to celestial navigation, long distance cruising, and other classes. Plus, you will have to make plans for financial independence during the four or five years it will take to make this trip.

Write down what you have to do to achieve your goals. This is a process, nothing happens overnight, and you <u>can</u> make it work! You know the steps involved in getting to where you want to go. And if you don't, then you need to investigate and find out what the steps are. Life doesn't happen by itself; you have to make it happen. So go out and do it.

Luck or Work

Did you know if you flip a coin in the air it will come up heads 50% of the time, and tails the other 50%? Now just imagine being at a carnival throwing baseballs at a bottle, blindfolded and 20 feet from your target. You start throwing and sooner or later you're going to hit the target. And if you keep on throwing, at some point you'll hit the bottle. This has nothing to do with luck. If you think positively and keep on trying, sooner or later you will win.

But if you stand in front of a full-length mirror, looking at yourself, and the first thing that comes to mind is a negative thought, what chance do you have at succeeding in life? The bullets of life are thoughts, and if you think you can hit the target—you will!

By taking off your blindfold, moving in close, and practicing your throwing, your chances of hitting the bottle will increase. So no matter where you go or what you do, it is not luck, it has only to do with you.

Now stand in front of a full-length mirror and look at yourself in the nude. What are the first thoughts that come to your mind? These are your predominate thoughts about yourself. Are they positive thoughts or negative thoughts? Do this exercise and write down your reaction and your thoughts.

- _____

- _____

- _____

Now take these thoughts and look at them. Are they positive? If not, what can you say to refute what your mind just told you about yourself? You know it really isn't true; we just get in the habit of putting ourselves down. *Now is the time to look on the bright side and tell yourself why those negative thoughts about you are not true. List your answers here.*

- _____

- _____

- _____

What Do You Think Happens?

What do you think happens when a child is constantly told he is a loser? What do you think this child will grow up to be if all he hears is that he is good for nothing and worse? Most of the time he grows up to fulfill the prophecy. This could be what has happened to you! You may have repeated negative thoughts to yourself for years and now you are living proof of the prophecy. It is time to change all of this, time to change the little words you hear in the back of your brain. There is always time to change and become the person you want to be. But how do you do it? The same way you got to this point: self-talk. But instead, start telling yourself positive and wonderful things about your *self*, or in the new age terminology,

53

"affirmations." Yes, affirmations do work whether they are positive or negative. You are living proof that they do.

Take the time to write out a list of affirmations to repeat to yourself. Write out things that are important to you. If you have low self-esteem, tell yourself you are a wonderful person and you deserve all the good things life has to offer. Write all of these affirmations in the present tense and use only positive words. The unconscious mind automatically resists negative phrases that begin with "I am not" or "I will not." Instead, you hear just the opposite of what you wanted for an affirmation such as, "I am not going to smoke." It ends up as. "I am going to smoke." Instead, use "I am a loving and caring person," or "I deserve all the good things in life," or "I am wealthy."

Create your own personal affirmations that fit your life based on what you said to yourself as you looked in the mirror.

Say these affirmations as often as possible. Stare deeply into your eyes while looking into a mirror and say your affirmations aloud. Say them over and over again in your mind. Many people find it is very hard to look deep within their own eyes. Some people start to laugh and think it is silly and walk away. Others start to cry. Still others get mad and walk away saying, "This is crazy." When we look deep within our eyes, we look deep within our soul. It is very hard to look within ourselves; it is easier to look at others.

Affirmations will start to work in about three to six months. The more often you say them, the faster they will work. You don't have to believe they will work to get started. Just do it anyway and after a while you will start to believe. It is not easy at first but keep up the good work and it will be weworth the time and effort. Your life will change for the better if that is what you really want. Use the affirmation "I allow myself to change every day and I'm moving forward in life." This affirmation will allow you to open up to change, so that other affirmations can be accepted.

Make a list of four affirmations you want for your life.

1._____

2._____

3._____

4._____

Now using your own voice, make a tape of these affirmations and play this tape just before you go to bed and any other possible time. Listening to your affirmations in your own voice affirms that you really do want to make these changes and helps you move forward towards becoming the person of your dreams.

Dreams plus discipline can make your life become totally different.

Now take the time to make your affirmation tape.

Stress Management

1. **Do you get upset over the little things in life?**
2. **Are you taking antacids all the time?**
3. **Do people push your buttons on a regular basis?**
4. **Do you feel like you are being thrown to the lions?**
5. **Is life overwhelming?**
6. **Do you have a hard time sleeping at night?**

What is Stress?

Stress is the inability of a person to adjust to all of life's demands placed on him or her, with subsequent biological and psychological responses to the demands.

Stress is a normal part of our daily lives. Because of that we have to learn to handle with stress in the right way. Unchecked stress allows disease to step in and take over our bodies by lowering our immune system.

Society is moving at a much faster pace now and this means we are bombarded with stressful events more often than in the past. In days gone by, we could use brut force and our ability to run fast to get us away from our stresses such as wild animals chasing us. That's not possible now because the stresses that we are dealing with are an intrigal part of our lives. We can't run away from our spouse, our boss, our children, the IRS or any number of situations that come up in our lives.

We have to learn to negotiate through stress in a positive manner by making changes in our lives and our perspective so we can see our challenges in a different light. Running away from a problem will never solve a problem, it will only get worse if we do. Sometimes we have to make decisions and choose between things that are not always pleasant. But making a choice also helps us to reduce stress.

What is the proper way to handle stress? The best way is with a positive frame of mind.

Whether we think of a glass as being half full rather than half empty gives us an idea of our kind of thinking. If we look really closely though, the glass is never empty. Something always fills the glass, either water or air. Letting go of wishful thinking and blame is also very instrumental in alleviating stress.

How Do You Know If You Have Stress?

Here's a simple test to find your stress level. Put a check mark (✓) next to those that apply to you. At the end of the test are directions on how to score your results. On the average most people don't want to admit they have stress. They think if they admit they are stressed, it means they can't handle life. But on the contrary, once we admit we have stress we can then change our life before stress does permanent damage to our mind, body and spirit.

Chuck Thurman of *Coast Weekly Magazine* (2000) in a recent article talks about *Prevention Magazine's* study on how stressed the public is. In 1985, 20% of the public felt they had overwhelming stress and in 1996, 73% of the public felt they had overwhelming stress. This means stress is going up at the rate of 4.81% a year.

If you project this out for the next six years soon we will all feel overwhelmed and stressed to the max.

This is a compilation of many different tests results and procedures, and some of my own devising, to find the ultimate in stress tests. I honestly feel this is the best stress test there is—but no test will really give an understanding of a person's stress. Only the individual himself knows when and for what reasons they are feeling overwhelmed with stress. In fact, I don't believe in tests— but the test below will give you a general idea of how you're doing. Many people can score very low on a stress test and at the same time feel overwhelmed with stress. Talking with your stress management therapist will give you a better idea of where you are at stress-wise.

Physical Signs of Stress

1. Increased cholesterol level in your blood (detected from blood test)
2. High blood pressure
3. Rapid pulse
4. Loss of appetite
5. Leg cramps
6. Tendency to overeat (especially in response to stressful situations)
7. Queasiness or butterflies in your stomach
8. Nausea
10. Heartburn
11. Eyestrain and headaches
12. Fluttering motions in your eyes
13. Tightened muscles in your neck
14. Grinding your teeth

15. Clenching your jaw
16. Cold hands
17. Sweaty palms
18. Contraction and tightness of general body muscles
19. Jerky movement
20. Weight loss or gain
21. Loss of voice
22. Tightness in your jaw
23. Shallow breathing
24. Strained sounding voice
25. Hunched over posture
    (resulting from excessive tightness of shoulder muscles)
26. Rigid spine, preventing fluid movement
    Tight forehead muscles, causing a change in facial expression
27. Contraction of the muscles in your fingers and toes, causing them to curl
28. Muscular pain (especially back pain)
29. Twitching and trembling
30. Dryness in your mouth
31. Lack of interest in sex
32. Frigidity
33. Impotence
34. Menstrual disorders
35. Nervousness
    (including the tendency to be frightened or startled easily)
36. Excessive belching
37. Chronic diarrhea
38. Chronic constipation
39. Chronic indigestion (including belching, heartburn, and nausea)
40. Weakness and fatigue

41. Eating junk food all the time
42. Dizziness
43. Fainting easily
44. Working all the time
45. Fainting spells preceded by nausea
46. Difficulty falling asleep
47. Inability to remain asleep during the night
48. Inability to sit still
49. Tendency to tire easily
50. Muscle spasms
51. Emotional eating
52. Excessive sleeping
53. Feeling full all the time without eating
54. Inability to cry
55. Drinking lots of coffee
56. Tendency to burst into tears at slight provocation or for no reason at all

Mental Signs of Stress

1. Depression
2. Irritability
3. Constant worry
4. Weak memory
5. Having accidents all the time
6. Intruding thoughts
7. Racing thoughts
8. Forgetfulness
9. The desire to escape from people or things or situations
10. Feeling like you want to cry

11. Impulsive behavior that is incompatible with normal patterns of behavior
12. Feelings of anxiety, sometimes vague or ill-defined
13. Paper shuffling
14. Inability to think clearly
15. Inability to solve simple problems
16. Lack of desire to participate fully in life
17. Feelings of self-destruction
18. Impatience
19. Being extremely critical of others
20. Meticulousness about surroundings and possessions
21. Tendency to be a perfectionist (everything has to be in its place)
22. Loose your temper frequently
23. Inability to relax physically (just can't let go)
24. Mild panic attacks
25. Frustration and concern over health (especially worries over minor aches and pains)
26. Fear of death
27. Fear of disease (especially cancer)
28. Fear of insanity or mental illness
29. Fear of being alone
30. Inability to cope with criticism
31. Inability to get along with others
32. Inability to concentrate
33. Feeling of separation or removal from people and things that were once important and vital
34. Tendency to live in the past
35. Feeling bored often
36. Feeling of inability to cope with problems and frustrations

37. Inability to freely express emotion, especially anger
38. Feeling your family members don't like or love you
39. Feeling of failure as a parent
40. Inability to confide problems or concerns with other people

Life Change Stress

1. Change in your sleep habits
2. Change in your recreation habits
3. Change in your social activities
4. Change in your financial state
5. Loss of a loved one
6. Loss of a friend
7. Divorce
8. Loss of a job
9. Having to commute
10. Trouble with relatives
11. Sexual problems
12. Health problems
13. Moved your household
14. Time in jail
15. Violations of the law
16. Changes in your business
17. Marriage
18. Graduation from college
19. Family member leaving home
20. Retirement
21. Changes in home environment
22. Vacation
23. Taking out a loan

Spiritual Stress

1. Feeling like there is no purpose to life
2. Uninspired
3. No goals and direction in life
4. Feeling alone
5. Very cynical about everything
6. Living life without dreams
7. Feeling alienated from everyone

How stressed are you?

The number of symptoms you experience consistently from day to day can be an important indicator of your stress levels. This table is meant to give you a general idea only. To derive more accurate   assessment of your level of stress, seek professional assistance. Any one of these symptoms may be sufficient cause for concern, or cause for no concern at all. We are all unique.

Here is some space to make a few notes about what you check off during this stress test.

- _____

- _____

- _____

- _____

Number of Life Stress Symptoms	Number of Physical Symptoms	Number of Mental Symptoms	Number of Spiritual Symptoms	Results
1 - 6	1 - 9	1- 6	0	Healthy
7 - 11	10 - 19	7 - 12	0 - 1	Reduce Stress
12 - 16	20 - 29	13 - 19	1 - 2	Major Changes
17 - 20	30 - 39	20 - 26	2 -	Find Help
21+	40+	27+	5+	Overwhelming

What Can I Do to Make A Change in My Life?

What you eat and drink as well as anything you ingest, has a tremendous effect on your body. Some foods help alleviate stress while others make it worse.

Foods That Soothe

"The Chinese believe that some foods have the ability to expand and allow us to relax, while others make us contract or tense. It is a mixture of the two types of foods, relaxing and tensing, that really allows us to relax deeply. There needs to be a balance between these foods in order to lessen stress" (The Relaxation Company, 1994).

Proteins are the precursors to brain chemicals like tryptophan, a calming agent. But proteins are also precursors for tyrosine and phenylalanine that help make adrenaline, an alertness chemical.

When consumed, protein first releases tyrosine and phenylalanine; tryptophan seems to lag behind. When proteins are consumed with whole grain carbohydrates, they stimulate insulin production, allowing more tryptophan uptake by the brain, thus relaxing the body. Large amounts of low or no-fiber carbohydrate food seem to induce sleepiness and lethargy. So it is important to use whole grain carbohydrates to slow the release of sugars into the system.

Large amounts of protein also seem to make a person feel sleepy and lethargic, so it is important to have a balanced diet.

Add Protein

To add protein to your diet in the morning, try egg whites, nonfat cream cheese, low fat peanut butter, soybean products like Gimelean (sausage) or tempeh to help balance the diet.

For lunch and dinner, chicken breast, turkey breast, seafood, tofu, tempeh and other proteins, and whole grain breads help to calm your day.

Stay Away From and Add

Try to stay away from caffeine (including chocolate), alcohol and salt as much as possible. These substances may keep us awake or make us feel relaxed at first, but later they make us feel tense. In fact, coffee and alcohol may induce anxiety or panic attacks.

"Onions are a mild sedative. Red and yellow onions were used for years by the Egyptians to induce relaxation.

Selenium may improve moods. Try foods high in selenium such as sunflower seeds, oysters, swordfish and clams.

Aromatic foods such as mild curries, cloves, cinnamon and nutmeg seem to be calming.

Complex carbohydrates should be in the form of whole grains and breads, such as whole-wheat pasta, oatmeal, brown rice, quinoa, polenta, popcorn, grits, and yams. Refined flour and sugar speed glucose to the brain, causing a burst of energy, possible tension and, finally, a sugar low. Yams are great because they have a low glycemic index, meaning they break down into sugars very slowly and give long-lasting energy without the sugar lows."(TRC, 1994)

What Happened to Lunch Breaks?

One of the main reasons people get on edge is that their blood sugar drops and they need to eat? In parts of Europe, a two or three hour lunch is normal. But Americans eat hastily in all kinds of places including in our cars, or going down the street to a fast food counter.

Many times we don't eat lunch at all. Perhaps it is time for Americans to enjoy the mid-day meal so we can live longer, happier lives.

Take the time to prepare foods that relax you, so you can enjoy them throughout the day. Freeze meals and then pop them in the microwave for a quick meal.

What is Relaxing All About?

Relaxing allows us to change from our major brain wave of Beta, to an Alpha, Theta, or Delta brain wave. We have 4 major brain wave patterns:

- Beta - Normal Waking State

- Alpha - Relaxation Brain Wave

- Theta - Dream State

- Delta - Restorative Sleep

Here are my own personal brain wave scans while in the waking state, then during meditation, self-hypnosis and lastly while listening to binaural beat music. As you can see there are marked differences in all these scans. Relaxation allows us to slow down our brain wave activity as much as possible. The flatter the EEG waves on the scan the more profound the feeling of relaxation. In order to deeply relax we have to shift our major brain wave from Beta to Alpha.

Normal EEG Scan

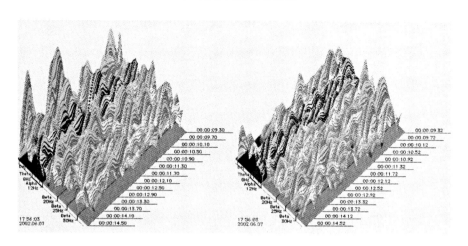

Meditation EEG Scan

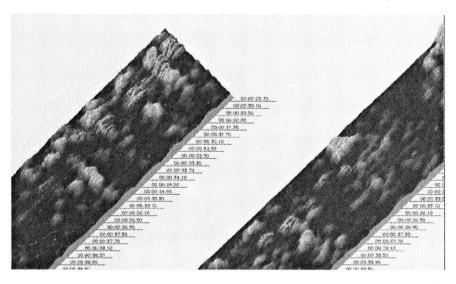

Self Hypnosis EEG Scan

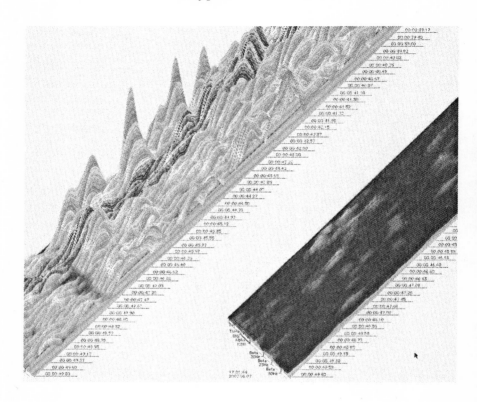

Binaural Beat Music EEG Scan

Here are a few ways to reach an Alpha brain wave state:

Music for Relaxation

Music has been used for years to control our feelings at events. Upbeat music with an energetic beat often causes people to get up and dance; it excites and energizes.

For relaxation, quieter music that is repetitive and doesn't have a specific beat is soothing.

If you take a soft-boiled egg to a rock concert and set it on the edge of the stage, by the time the concert is over, it will harden, because loud noise has been found to coagulate protein. So what does loud noise do for our bodies and minds? If the egg is any indication about what loud noise can do, I'm staying home and avoiding those harmful effects!

There are all types of relaxing music: New Age, Classical, World/Ethnic and Light Jazz. Personal taste in music plays a big role. Some people find soft rock relaxing, and classical music lovers might prefer listening to Mozart. Choose what works for you. Whatever the type of music, just breathe it in and let it relax your muscles and nerves.

Some of the most relaxing sounds are sounds from nature. Many of us hear a call to return to nature, and the sound of a cooing dove or a trickling stream can be very relaxing. The ocean, with its crashing waves, induces relaxation. If you can't hear it from where you are, you can get it on CD or tape.

Whatever the music, try to stay away from music with a distinctive beat. Otherwise, the beat takes over our minds and all we think about is the beat. But in certain instances a beat can be good.

Indian drumming or our own heartbeat has the ability to carry us far away to another place and keep our minds away from our daily thoughts.

Binaural beat music is another very relaxing type of music, which is best listened to with stereo headphones. While listening to Binaural beat music specific tones are created for both the right and left ear. Because of the specialized frequencies created (Tones) the brain in turn creates another tone (third tone) which is very relaxing. I find this type of music very soothing and delightful. Binaural beat music also has been used successfully to help people with all kinds of conditions including, stress, ADD, recovery from brain trauma and many other types of health challenges. If you have any questions about binaural beat music or would like to experience this wonderful relaxing technique contact:

Professor Alejandro Jose' at the Instituto Psicosonia, Inc., P.O. BOX 6728, San Juan, Puerto Rico, USA 00914-6728 email psicosonia@caribe.net or phone 787-728-5372.

Here are a few of my favorite pieces of music:

Harmonic Resonance – Jim Oliver
Let the Ocean Worry – Fred Weinberg and Joe Beck
Garden of Dreams – Aki Akbar Khan
Ocean Dreams – Dean Evenson
Higher Ground –Steven Halpern
Sedona Suite –Tom Barabas
Lost Oceans – John Huling
Seven Wheels of Light – Joel Andrews

Wind & Mountain – Deuter

Ocean Beach – Miramar

Hawaiian Slack Key Guitar — Dancing Cat Records

In the Key of Healing – Steven Halpern

Inner Dance – Dr. Jeffery Thompson

The Fairy Ring – Mike Rowland

Tear of the Moon – Coyote Oldman

Eternity II, A Romantic Collection – Real Music

Pachelbel's Canon – Pachelbel–Leppard

Adagio for Strings, Op. II – Samuel Barber

Changes – Carlos Nakai

Plenitud—Alejandro Jose'

Any of the Series of Music by the Relaxation Company

Color can Lower Your Stress Level

Color is everywhere; many different tints and hues surround us. Color can have a psychological and physical effect on us. It affects our emotions, our levels of stress, our blood pressure and the way we look at the world. In general, light colors help us feel relaxed and dark shades may cause us to feel oppressed and reduce the feeling of space.

Red	Very uplifting; stimulating; stimulates the appetite; can also increase blood pressure or cause anxiety.
Orange	Same qualities as red.

Yellow   Uplifting; very stimulating; nice in a work area; not relaxing enough for a bedroom.

Green   Has the ability to calm; is suitable for most rooms; soothing and relaxing; tends to remind us of soothing outdoor scenes.

Blue   Creates a spacious feeling; very relaxing and calming; can lower blood pressure; a great color for bedrooms.

Lilac/
Lavender   Warming; peaceful; relaxing; dark shades can be depressing.

Black   Very impressive; depressing; was used for brain washing in the past

White   Very spacious feeling; peaceful; relaxing; can keep one alert at the same time. (Time-Life, 1997)

Greens and blues are probably the most common relaxing colors, with lavender and purple close seconds. The rest is up to you. What color would you wear to a dinner party you are feeling uptight about? Perhaps not red. But if you were feeling excited and energetic, that red shirt or dress might be just the thing.

Breath

Shallow breathing is often associated with muscle tension, headaches, fatigue, depression, anxiety disorder, migraines, panic attacks, agoraphobia, and I believe it has a lot to do with heart attacks. The first muscle deprived of oxygen when we hold our breath when we are stressed is the heart.

Breathing can be one of the most relaxing things we can do for ourselves. How many times in the middle of something nerve-racking have you found yourself unable to breathe? When we get stressed we breathe very shallowly or hold our breath. Interestingly, this is just the opposite of what we should do. Whenever we take a deep breath and let it out, we feel a little tension flow away. When we take in more oxygen, our minds and bodies function at their peak capacity. Breathing is something we control, but at the same time It is not completely in our control. If I hold my breath, I'll eventually pass out and start to breathe again. Breathing is an involuntary process within our bodies over which we have partial voluntary control.

If you watch a newborn baby, you'll notice that the abdomen moves up and down with each breath; this is our normal way of breathing. But over the years we learn to breathe very shallowly, decreasing the amount of oxygen we take in. Many of us are trained to hold our stomachs in, resulting in shallow breathing. Constrictive clothing can also keep us from breathing deeply, so loosen up that belt.

Take a deep breath all the way down to your abdomen, and let your abdomen expand as you inhale. Feel your breath filling you up, all the way up to your neck and shoulders. As you exhale, your abdomen contracts. Take a few moments to practice correct breathing.

Have you been a shallow breather in the past?

Yes_____ No_____

Become aware of your breath. Notice anything that causes you to stop breathing or to start breathing very shallowly. By noticing what stops our breathing we can identify the events, issues and ideas that tend to cause us stress and work on resolving them.

Now take the time to write down a diary of what emotions, events and situations cause you to breathe shallowly. Do this exercise for a week and note what seems to cause you stress. Can these situations be avoided, changed, or revised in a positive way? Write your response below.

- _____

- _____

- _____

- _____

If you find yourself holding your breath on a regular basis, try setting the alarm on your watch to go off every fifteen minutes to remind you to take a deep breath.

How the Voice can Calm

Voice is our inner instrument for music. With each word we speak and every note we sing our whole body vibrates with tones that heal.

Could this be why, down through time, Gregorian Monks, Tibetan Monks or Indians of the New World have chanted? Chanting is found in almost every country and society in the world. Be it reciting Hail Mary's, counting prayer beads, or chanting the deep two-toned chants of the monks of Nepal, all chants bring about healing.

Healing starts with the ability to relax and let go. With relaxation, muscles allow the capillaries to fill and move vital nutrients to areas of need throughout the body.

Have you ever noticed when you're not feeling well, perhaps when you have the stomach flu, that you automatically let out a moan or a sigh? It seems as though this sound helps your stomach to feel better. People have been chanting those same kinds of sounds for years.

Gregorian Monks have a very long work schedule and chant for eight hours a day, and sleep a very short period of time. They attribute their stamina and hard-working ability to the chanting they do everyday.

The sounds of *"Om"* and *"Ahh"* just seem to make us feel better and let out tensions that get stored up in the body. The next time you feel a little down, try chanting the sounds *Om* and *Ahh*, and see what happens.

Take the time to write down your reaction the next time you're not feeling well, and try chanting Om or Ahh for ten or fifteen minutes. Did you feel better afterwards?

- _____

- _____

- _____

The Benefits of Walking

Taking a few minutes out of your busy day to walk can release pent-up tension. But taking the time to breathe, walk and fully relax can do wonders for you.

I have a friend who, with the help of a simple walking exercise and breathing, lost over 100 pounds. He started out just walking along at a slow rate, noticing his breath. Then he switched his concentration to each footfall in a very deliberate way. He noticed everything it took to move one leg and take a step, and then move the next leg and take a step, and so on. Let your mind be totally absorbed in the action of walking, and you'll feel more relaxed.

A runner can also use this with running or jogging, counting footfalls during the course of a run. Just let your mind be totally immersed in the counting footfalls, letting all the rest of your thoughts be acknowledged as they come to you. Then say to yourself, "Yes, I acknowledge these thoughts, but not right now," and let them go. Continue to count footfalls and let your thoughts go. This works very well and has been used by hundreds of thousands of people to help them relax. In fact I have another friend who runs five miles every morning, counting to himself as he runs, letting go of thoughts which allow his day to go much better.

Try Deliberate Walking or Running and write down your reaction below. Was this a good process? Did you find that your mind stopped thinking about your worries?

- _____

- _____

- _____

The Sense of Smell

Have you ever noticed a particular smell and suddenly been carried off to another place and time? For me, this happens every time I smell a cigar. I automatically find myself thinking of the county fair where I grew up in Woodland, California. With the smell of a fresh cut field of hay, I'm whisked away out to the field with my dad, who was a farmer in the valley.

The olfactory lobe in our brain has an amazing amount of interaction with the rest of our body.

Since ancient times, fragrant oils and perfumes have been used to relax and help heal. The Egyptians, Greeks, East Indians, Arabs and Native Americans all have used essential oils to relax and heal.

"When a fragrance is inhaled, the information travels from the nose to the limbic system in the brain, where it triggers memories and influences physical and emotional behavior. Olfactory stimulation can start the production of hormones, influence appetite, and change body temperature, metabolism, stress levels and sex drive. Smells can also influence our immune system and our thoughts. Fragrances can evoke physiological and psychological responses to the environment by stimulating the release of neurotransmitters and endorphins in your brain, which produce an over-all sense of well being. The endorphins and neurotransmitters can bring about sexual feelings, reduce stress, relieve pain and restore and relax." (The Relaxation Company, 1994).

The Formal Name for this is Aromatherapy.

How can we use aromatherapy? Take a time-out bath with essential oils. Light aromatherapy candles. Use skin and body care products that have soothing scents. Have a massage with essential oils, or use an essential oil diffuser to fill your home with relaxing scents.

There are up to a hundred different essential oils on the market. Choose the ones you like the most and seem to be relaxing to you. Here is a short list of some of the most common scents for relaxing.

Cedarwood	Chamomile	Clary Sage	Elemi
Fennel	Frankincense	Geranium	Jasmine
Juniper	Lavender	Marjoram	Neroli
Orange	Palmarosa	Patchouli	Rose
Rosemary	Rosewood	Sandalwood	Thyme
Vetiver	Ylang Ylang		

Take a time-out bath with scented candles and essential oils in the water and ask Mom or Dad to take care of the kids. Give yourself thirty minutes to relax and indulge yourself. Write down your feelings during and afterwards. Was it relaxing?

- _____

- _____

- _____

Yoga! Ever Notice How Cats are so Relaxed?

When a cat wakes up from a nap it normally stretches its whole body, very slowly. Have you ever held a cat's leg and noticed just how soft the muscles are, but at the same time very strong and agile? Maybe there's something to this stretching. Could it be that stretching allows us to let go of muscular tensions that build up throughout the day?

Yoga can release tension, helping you let go of stress. Yoga also stresses breath work. There must be something to this breathing idea, or it would not be so important in so many different disciplines.

With yoga, the abdominal breath is very important. Remember that we stop breathing or breathe shallowly when we get stressed, so breathing deeply allows us to let go of some of that pent-up stress. This is what yoga is all about: relaxing, stretching and concentrating on breathing.

Take twenty minutes a day and feel your breath come in through your nose all the way down to your abdomen. Then exhale and feel the breath move from the abdomen out through the nose or mouth. Just concentrate on the activity of breathing, and eventually the long slow exhalation will be a perfect, natural tranquilizer.

Together with a few simple stretches, this yoga program has the ability to do away with a lot of the stress that life entails.

Find a comfortable, warm place. Wear loose clothing and no shoes. Take the telephone off the hook and let everyone in the house know this is your time and you are not to be disturbed.

Eat at least thirty minutes prior to your yoga session or at least thirty minutes after. Take thirty seconds between each stretch and breath deeply. Be sure to consult with your doctor about any health problems before starting yoga.

Here are some simple yoga poses you can start with today. Go slowly! Yoga can cause people to be a bit sore. To start with, don't stretch beyond your comfort level.

Pose 1. Breathing

Sit on a chair with your feet flat on the floor and breathe deeply, using the abdominal breathing technique described previously.

Pose 2. Head Rolls

Take in a breath. Exhale and allow your head to tilt toward your right shoulder. As you inhale, straighten your head. Exhale as you tilt your head toward your left shoulder, and then inhale and straighten your head again. Then exhale as you bend your head forward, inhale as you lift and straighten it again.

Pose 3. Shoulder Shrugs

Inhale, raising your shoulders up to your ears. Then exhale slowly while you let your shoulders drop. Do this five or six times, being sure to exhale slowly when letting the shoulders down. Be sure to move your shoulders only within your comfort range.

Pose 4. The Cat Stretch

Inhale, raising both arms up toward the ceiling, then exhale slowly. In the next move, yawn and stretch one arm up toward the ceiling. Then inhale and do the same for the other side. Do this a couple of times for both sides. Be careful not to over-stretch your lower back.

Pose 5. Bear Hug

Sitting down, give yourself a big hug as you exhale. Then inhale and release your hold allowing yourself to relax. Do this exercise three or four times.

Pose 6. Reach for the Sky

In your chair, inhale and then exhale, reaching for the sky with both hands, stretching out your shoulders and upper back. Inhale and relax, allowing yourself to release any tension in your body. Repeat three or four times.

Pose 7. Knee Up

In your chair, inhale and then exhale while pulling up one leg up with your hands close to your chest. Inhale and allow your leg to go back to its normal position. Repeat three or four times, alternating legs.

This can be a lot of fun at your desk…take the time to do this exercise and relax.

Pose 8. Repeat the breathing you did in Pose 1.

Of course, yoga can be much more involved and advanced than this, but it doesn't have to be. Just take twenty minutes a day to stretch and breathe, then you'll know why cats are so relaxed.

Other relaxing exercises you might also check out are Tai chi and Qi Qong.

Give yoga a try. What did you think? Did you feel more relaxed?

- _____

- _____

- _____

Sleep Stress

Sleep habits are something we learn, not something we are born with. Have you ever been so amped up that you had a hard time sleeping? Of course you have, we all have at one time or another. Do you have a regular routine of going to sleep at a set time? If not, you might think about the fact that our minds become accustomed to sleeping at a certain time. Also, our circadian rhythms (our natural rhythm of dark and light, daytime and nighttime) play a large part in how well we sleep. The pineal gland of the brain regulates the flow of melatonin. When it gets dark the pineal gland triggers a response, releasing melatonin into our bloodstream, telling our brain we feel tired and it is time to go to sleep. As we get older a little less melatonin is released, causing us to stay awake longer.

We think and worry about everything in the middle of the night. And of course worry and stress have a direct response upon our brain and our endocrine system, causing everything to be affected and thrown off balance.

Good sleep habits start with staying away from sugar, caffeine, alcohol, chocolate and other stimulants in general. Also it is hard to sleep on a full stomach, so make sure you eat your last meal at least 2 hours before going to bed. Make a list of things you need to do just before going to bed so you won't have to be disturbed by such things as, "Oh no, I forgot to put the cat out."

Go to bed at the same time each night. Shut off the TV one hour before going to bed, and no television in bed—that's a real no-no; television only keeps your mind going. Never eat in bed; keep your bedroom a special place for sleeping. Make it a place of peace and solitude. Paint your bedroom a nice soothing light blue, green or lavender. These are the most relaxing colors for enhancing sleep.

Read something soothing and relaxing, putting your mind at ease before you go to bed. Be thankful for the day you've had, and say out loud to yourself all the nice things that have happened to you today. This will help you relax your mind and allow you to know everything is O.K. Think positive thoughts about what will happen tomorrow, and allow tomorrow to unfold in the morning. In India, it is said that our sleep connects us with our Golden Inner Light that keeps our soul alive. Remember to connect with that inner peace every night.

So start some new sleep habits with a few of the tips I've given you here. Most of all, don't take sleep for granted, we all need rest and relaxation. It is not about being lazy or not accomplishing anything. On the contrary, we are allowing our body to rejuvenate and be replenished so we can feel great tomorrow. Your body will appreciate it, and you will have a whole new outlook on life.

Need a Vacation and Can't Afford it?

There are alternatives to this dilemma. One is to just sit back in a nice comfortable chair in a place where you won't be disturbed. Close your eyes and just imagine a beautiful rose in front of you. Imagine this rose turning around slowly and notice the velvety texture of the petals, so delicate and soothing. Notice the way the petals curve outward. The ruby color of each petal is like beautiful rich red velvet cloth. See the color of the stem, the way the leaves branch out, the little veins in each shiny leaf so detailed. As the rose turns slowly in front of you, take a deep breath and breathe in the aroma of the rose, so delicate and light and wonderful. As you take another deep breath of this wonderful relaxing fragrance, just imagine the aroma beginning to swirl like a cloud around and into your head, relaxing everything it comes in contact with.

Allow this cloud to move down your neck, allow your neck to relax and just let go, then feel the cloud move down to your shoulders and let them droop and relax. Let the cloud of relaxing aroma move on down your arms and through your elbows and then through your lower arms, down through your wrists and hands and on out through your fingertips. Just imagine it relaxing your chest and then flowing on down to your abdomen, relaxing all your internal organs. Imagine this cloud relaxing all of your back muscles so they feel very heavy. Feel the cloud roll down your hips, relaxing and soothing them, and down your legs, letting them feel loose and lazy. Then finally down to your knees and your calves. It is so nice to relax and just let go. Let it flow down through your ankles and into your feet where the cloud soothes and massages your feet. Allow a very peaceful feeling to flow throughout your whole body. It is so nice to relax and to allow yourself to have that wonderful gift of deep relaxation. Now take a nice, long, deep breath and when you're ready, slowly open your eyes.

Welcome to Creative Visualization and a Short Vacation

Other names for this technique are *meditation* or *self-hypnosis*. It is a very simple technique of visualizing in order to promote deep relaxation, and can also be combined with relaxing specific areas of the body that might be very tight and stiff (for instance, when your neck feels like a steel girder). Allow your breath to help you relax and let all your tension and stiffness flow away.

At the National Institute of Health, studies were done with runners visualizing running a race. With very sophisticated equipment the researchers were able to detect very small contractions of the runners' muscles, as though they were actually running. So if what we see in our mind makes a change in our bodies, what do you think would happen if you visualized relaxing? You're right! The muscles of the neck and shoulders, or wherever tension is being held, start to relax and a feeling of well being starts to set in.

Make a tape of these words in your own voice and listen to it just before you go to bed it will help you sleep deeply.

Give this technique a try. What did you feel during this process? Write down your experience below.

• _____

• _____

- _____

- _____

Fall Asleep Easily and Effortlessly!

Do this same routine of visualizing the rose just before going to bed. Another technique of relaxing into sleep at night is to progressively tighten and relax all the parts of your body from your feet all the way up to the top of your head. Breathe deeply, concentrate on your breathing, and whenever any thoughts pull you away, just acknowledge them. Say to yourself, " not right now," and go back to concentrating on your breath. You'll soon find you are sleeping soundly.

What Natural Remedies Can I Buy Over The Counter to Help Me Relax?

There are lots of old remedies that work very well. For instance, Chamomile tea has been around for ages and has a very relaxing and soothing effect on the body. Another remedy is Kombu tea, seaweed that is brewed into a tea. It is very soothing for the nerves. Shiso leaves can be boiled into a tea, which is also very soothing.

When our grandparents came home from working in the fields they were dead tired and they had no problem going to sleep. Exercise is very important. It releases endorphins that give us a feeling of well being, allowing us to sleep. Many times our jobs don't provide us with much physical exercise. So the fatigue we feel is emotional, and running, jogging, playing tennis or whatever else we enjoy helps us let go of some of the emotional baggage that gets in the way of sleeping at night. Just be sure to exercise several hours before retiring, not just beforehand or it will keep you awake.

Of course, there are lots of herbs that can help you relax and let go of stress, such as Ginseng, Golden Seal and Kava Kava. I would recommend that you talk with a knowledge able herbalist. They can give you important information on herbs, their uses and interactions. Here are a few well-known anti-stress herbs:

Oriental Ginseng	Goldenseal	Hops
Catnip	Valerian	Passion Flower
Hawthorn Berries	St. Johns Wort	Chamomile
Skullcap	Black Cohash	Cayenne
Garlic		

After going to your local herbalist, list below which types of herbs work for you.

- _____

- _____

Massage

Therapeutic massage has been around for thousands of years, and is very popular throughout the world. In Turkey, warm-water massage consists of regular massage with buckets of warm water poured over you every now and then – very relaxing.

Touch is one of the most healing of all modalities, according to Andrew Weil. Babies actually die if they don't receive loving kindness in the way of touch. A study was done in which some babies were touched on a regular basis and some were not. The babies who were touched gained weight at a much faster rate than the ones not touched. So, it seems that loving touch is very important for optimum health. (Weil, 1995)

Ten minutes of gently massaging a painful, stress-filled neck can make a world of difference. Massage, together with visualization, aromatherapy and stretches, can literally melt stress away.

Take the time to give your significant other a massage and have him or her give you a massage. Write down what you felt like after your massage.

- _____

- _____

New Technologies for Relaxation

Some new technologies used for relaxation are Biofeedback and Light-Sound machines. Biofeedback uses sophisticated electronic instruments that can help you develop the ability to relax. Electroencephalographs (EEG), Galvanic skin response meters (GSR) and Electromyography meters (EMG) are used to help one develop the ability to relax all parts of the body. As you relax, the instruments give you feedback on how you are progressively relaxing. There are three certified biofeedback centers in my area, and some small biofeedback machines for home use are available by mail order.

Light-Sound machines are devices that use a recording and a set of glasses containing flickering LED lights. These lights coincide with the music and help you drift away, letting go of all thoughts and stress. Light-Sound machines work very well and allow you to relax very deeply. Light-Sound machines can be obtained through mail-order catalogs.

Note: People with a history of epilepsy or seizures should not use these machines.

Give one of these new technological devices a try and write down your experience below.

- _____

- _____

How Magnets Lower Stress Levels

I want tell you the story of a woman who for years had back problems. She lives on the East Coast and went through surgery and every imaginable treatment in order to stop the pain. She couldn't even lean over the bathroom sink without cringing in pain.

She became depressed and started to wonder about life. Her husband had a very high paying job so she was able to stay home and take care of the kids. But even being home, the pain was unbearable.

Then one day someone in her neighborhood asked her to try a magnetic back belt. She thought to herself, "This will never work," and said, "No thanks." A month later she saw the same person again and he offered her the back belt again to use. So she decided oh what the heck, why not. She wore the belt around the house and to bed that night. Upon getting up the next morning she went to the bathroom sink, and out of habit bending over the sink, then it hit her, no pain. What happened?

All she could figure is that this magnetic belt had changed her body somehow. She didn't understand it. But there wasn't anything to understand, other than the fact that she was pain free!

It is theorized that magnetic fields change the movement of ions in cells, which could make pain receptors less sensitive, and increase oxygen transport. They increase capillary blood flow, which may promote healing. Magnets also increase the blood levels of pain killing endorphins and endorphins help us to feel relaxed and calm.

Many people will say that's a bunch of bunk. Well, it's not if you have been in pain for years. And just this morning a friend of mine told me of someone else with back pain that tried magnets and it made a difference.

I feel that in the near future magnets will be accepted therapy for pain. Even acupuncture has taken Western medicine a long time to see the benefits. I've even noticed players in the NBA wearing magnetic wraps. This may be the stress reducing solution for you.

The Stress of Pain—One Way to Eliminate it

Anytime we are in pain we are feeling stressed. As soon as you start to feel pain you automatically react with the fight or flight syndrome. You tense up, and your muscles are ready to run away from whatever is causing the pain. Adrenalines and cortisols are pumping throughout your body getting you ready to be able to do battle. But there is help!

Have you ever had the aches and pains of the flu or a cold and went out into the sun and soaked up those warm sunny rays? Of course you have. Just about everyone has done that at one time or another. You even see cats and dogs lying in the sun warming their bodies. Did you know those rays which warm your body are far infrared rays, and that those rays penetrate all the way through to your bones? Plus your body also gives off far infrared energy.

What if there was a way to warm your body with those warming rays without the bad effects of the carcinogenic rays of the sun? Well there is! There are some new space age fibers on the market that are made from the same material that the covering of the space shuttle and the spacesuits the astronauts wear are made of. As you know, when the space shuttle re-enters the earth's atmosphere there is tremendous heat built up around the shuttle and this ceramic material reflects the heat back into space. Also astronauts walking in space are subjected to extreme temperatures and this same material keeps them warm or cool throughout this whole process.

Because far infrared rays have the ability to penetrate through your entire body, they also have the ability to help increase healing at a deeper level. Heating pads only penetrate about one inch but this new material allows your own infrared heat to be reflected back in to help you heal. There is no need to plug it in, heat it up, or charge it up, all you do is wear this fiber and it warms the body sufficiently to increase circulation thus increasing healing.

I have been sleeping with a thin little comforter made of this material and it is amazing. I'm always the right temperature. If there are two people under one of these comforters and one sleeps warm and the other cold, both will sleep comfortably. And because of the ability to regulate your internal temperature to a much better degree and the increase in blood supply which increases internal warmth, your body's pH also has the ability to adjust faster than normal. When we exercise we have lactic acid which builds up in our tissues. This gives us aches and pains, and this far infrared material helps to move that acid out of our bodies at a much faster rate which helps us to feel comfortable.

Far infrared products used in combination with other health products such as magnetics, vitamins and nutritional supplements can help you to enjoy life with a significant decrease in your bodily stress.

News and Stress

How much positive information do we see on the news every night? Not much. Probably 98% of all news has to be high-impact, so disasters of all kinds seem to get everyone's attention. Sensationalism seems to have taken over the media. For every bad thing reported on the news, there are probably a thousand good things that happen every day.

I knew a woman who became so afraid of the world as a result of what she saw on the news every day, that she began to shut herself indoors, away from the world. I asked her if anything awful had taken place in her community and she said, "No, of course not." After showing her a few of the great things that happened every day in the few blocks around her home, she realized she was creating stress and tension she really didn't need by watching the news. Another man noticed that he arrived home from work every day irritable and anxious, for no apparent reason. When he stopped listening to the news on the radio on the way home from work, the irritability and anxiety disappeared.

If you're addicted or accustomed to watching or listening to the news and reading the newspaper every day and it causes you stress, Dr. Weil recommends weaning yourself off of it by giving up watching the news and reading the newspaper for one day the first week. The next week, give it up for two nights and the next week, three nights. Do this until the seventh week when you're no longer watching the news or reading the newspaper at all. (Weil, 1995)

At the end of eight weeks, you'll be amazed how much less stress you have in your life. If something really important happens that you *really* need to know about, someone you know is bound to tell you about it.

Give this eight week course a try and write down what you're feeling at the end of the eight weeks below.

- _____

- _____

- _____

The Importance of Relationships

Once there was an Italian community on the East Coast with a very low incidence of heart attacks. A group of researchers wanted to find out why, so they put the whole community through rigorous testing to determine why they had such healthy hearts. When all the results were in, they couldn't figure out a good reason why people in this community didn't have heart problems.

Then they started to notice the wonderful network of relationships in this town. Everyone always had someone to talk to and if they ever needed help, the whole town came to their rescue. They never had to worry because they knew no matter what happened someone would help them make it through the hard times.

Janice Kiecolt-Glaser, Ph.D., director of the division of Health Psychology at the Ohio State University College of Medicine in Columbus, has found that people having surgery who came from highly stressful family situations, healed much more slowly than people who had many healthy relationships. So it seems having good relationships with family and friends is paramount to reducing stress *(The Relaxation Company, 1994).*

97

How could you start to build a network of loving individuals in your life? Write some ideas below.

- _____

- _____

- _____

Pets Can Help You Feel Soothed and Calm

Have you ever noticed just how wonderful it is to pet a cat or dog? To just sit and stroke their coat and be totally loved by a wonderful animal? Pets love unconditionally compared to people. No matter what you do to your pet it will come back and still love you a few hours later. Pets are being brought into nursing homes to help sooth the anxiety of being old. Yes, pets can help you relax and let go of stress.

Sit down and stroke a pet for 20 minutes today and write down what you're feeling before and after this exercise.

- _____

- _____

Reduce Stress by Diving into Your Hobbies

Do you love to garden, cook, sail, hike, run, socialize or paint? There are so many hobbies I can't list them all here. Most people find their mind gets so deeply involved in what they are doing that their worries seem to slip away. Even the hours seem to fly by when you're busy with something you love to do. People with hobbies seem much more in balance, perhaps by having more to do than just working all the time. You can even make wonderful friends who enjoy the same hobbies as you do. It has also been documented that people who garden, for instance, are healthier. So dive into your hobbies, letting the worries of the world go for a few hours.

What hobbies do you have that let your mind slip away? Make a list below of old and new hobbies you enjoy or would like to start.

- _____

- _____

- _____

Another Way to Reduce Stress is to Tell Yourself You Are Relaxed

If a person goes around telling everyone he is a loser, what do you think is going to happen in his life? Right things are going to be very difficult for that person. It is sometimes said the only difference between a millionaire and a person who isn't a millionaire is the fact that the millionaire always thought he would be a millionaire. If a child is told over and over that he is worthless and useless, sooner or later that becomes his reality. So if you were to start telling yourself, "I am relaxed and calm at all times; I find peace in my breathing," perhaps you will start to believe and manifest it.

Affirmations like this one are very important! Whatever we tell ourselves every day easily becomes our reality. These are all self-fulfilling prophecies. I used to know someone who would tell himself he would get a cold every year at a certain time. And you know what—he *did* get a cold just as he said he would. How could he not? He had set up the whole event from the beginning.

Write down a simple statement to say to yourself every day that will be positive and allow you to relax.

- _____

- _____

- _____

Laugh Your Stress Away

Have you ever laughed to the point of having your sides hurt? Were you stressed when you finished? Of course not.

Little kids laugh at least forty times a day. How many times did you laugh today? Most adults laugh only five or six times a day. Laughing oxygenates your blood, increases endorphins in your blood stream, and helps you feel soothed and calm. Medical science has shown laughing will help you heal your mind and body. Life is not about being serious all the time. Joke, laugh, and have fun. Life is about enjoying every moment. Take a look around and you'll notice the people who laugh seem so much more lighthearted. Perhaps it is time to laugh, and enjoy this wonderful gift called life!

I was coming back from giving a seminar this morning when traffic slowed down to a crawl and then stopped. I wondered what was going on so I looked down the road and could see the traffic was being blocked by something. I then moved down the road until I could get a little closer to see what was going on. Then I burst out laughing. To my surprise it was a large group of Canadian geese crossing the road from the lake to some grass on the other side. The leader made the first step into the road and all the rest followed. Each goose was stepping right in time with the lead goose. It was amazing, I was thinking, *"If I didn't know better I would think they were all mesmerized by the lead goose, as though they were sleep walking."*

Then I looked around. While I was laughing and having a great time, other drivers were drumming impatiently, yelling at the geese, and scowling like the world had come to an end. What a difference. I was in a place of happiness, comfort and fun, and everyone else looked as though they had accidentally sat down on their false teeth. I started to think, *"What happened to them?"*

Then it hit me: *what a mind set difference we have.* Here I am watching one of the most amazing things I've seen in a long time and just cracking up, and the rest of the world is miserable. Whoa!

People are just too busy to take in the silliness of the universe. This little bit of fun was put right in front of their noses and they didn't even blink. Make sure you are not rushing around so fast that you miss out on how silly the world is. Life is full of all kinds of crazy stuff if we only open our eyes to see it.

In fact, I was walking near the ocean the other day and decided I needed to use the bathroom on my walk. So I walked down to a public restroom and into a stall which needed to be flushed, so I took care of it. All of a sudden water from the pipe above that supplied the toilet showered me in the most powerful stream of water I've ever been in. It was like getting hit with a fire hose. I was drenched and stunned! All I could do was walk out of the stall and start to laugh. I was soaked to the bone, but what was I to do? I just burst out laughing, and I couldn't help myself. Here I walked in to relieve myself—and I'll tell you, I totally forgot about using the facilities! A person walked in and asked me what was going on and I responded saying, "Well I wouldn't try the shower if I were you." Then I walked out and sat on a rock and sunned myself like a cormorant with outstretched wings sitting on a rock.

What more can I say? There are two ways of looking at life, one is stressful and the other is laughing at all the crazy things that happen in the universe. Now, how are you going to react to the next crazy thing that happens to you? It is your choice.

How many times did you laugh today? How are you going to remedy this problem? Write down how you can change your life so you can laugh more.

- _____

- _____

- _____

- _____

The Most Important Way to Relax

Changing your frame of mind to one of being grateful and positive about life makes a huge difference. Change your thoughts to abundance, knowing there is enough for everyone. Say to yourself, "I deserve to have all the good things in life." Perhaps start a gratitude journal and write down everything for which you are grateful. Then if you're feeling down, take a look at that journal and remind yourself of all the good things in life that you have.

Go out now and buy a book or journal for writing, and every evening just before going to bed, write down a list of things for which you are grateful. List every little thing, such as, "Good food", " someone said Thank You", the time you took for a nice bath, and so on.

The most important thing is to take time to just *be*. Take twenty to thirty minutes a day to allow yourself the gift of relaxation. We all deserve to relax, and perhaps it is time for you to allow yourself that wonderful gift.

The Mind/Body Interaction

What interaction does our mind and body have? Does it really matter what we think as long as we try to eat and exercise every day? These are questions I'm about to answer, and I think you will find the answers fascinating.

I also had an experience while out fishing in the Pacific Ocean. A few friends and I were going out bottom fishing from Bodega Bay. It was a rough sea that day and a good friend of mine put a scopolamine patch behind his ear to keep him from getting seasick. We were being bounced all around and things were getting wet. But my friend was enjoying himself and caught his limit of fish. About halfway through our trip I noticed my friend's scopolamine patch had fallen off. At this point he was fine and I didn't say a thing to him until hours later. Then I said, "Hey, your patch fell off hours ago," and he immediately turned a deep shade of green and started getting sick. I'll never forget that incident. It started me thinking about the power of our minds over our bodies.

That opens the door to mind/body interaction. Mind/body interaction is having an idea of what health is, and locking that idea in our subconscious. By doing a PET Scan (Positron Emission Tomography) on the brain, scientists have tested mind/body interaction. At the same time a nuclear scan of a person's brain was being done, the patient was asked to look at a photograph of nature. Doctors could see the areas of the brain that lit up while looking at the scene and the hormones that were going out to the organs of the body. When this very same person just remembered the nature scene, they showed the exact same areas of the brain reacting in the same way. So it goes to show, all we have to do is to remember something, and it will have the same effect on our bodies as the original scene.

If you have a dream or you're at the movies, what comes into your mind has a reaction in your body to a much greater extent than most people think or even want to believe. In fact I was in an amusement park ride in Los Angles riding in a futuristic car and looking at a I-Max screen while the car was tipped up and down, back and forth. By the end of the ride I really felt as though I had gone on a trip somewhere. This was a perception and not a reality. Again our mind has an ability to change our bodies, with either positive or negative effects.

This is the process by which virtual reality computer games work. These games are getting more and more realistic all the time. We are tricked into feeling what we are doing and feeling, hearing and sensing are real, but in reality it is just a perception, not reality itself.

Memories involving fear are permanently ingrained in our brains, causing all kinds of problems later in life.

For instance, there is a huge group of Laotians who died while sleeping, for no apparent reason. No cause was detected other than the fact that they all were under large amounts of stress. Some survivors told a story of sleeping normally, then suddenly not being able to move, and then not being able to breathe. Then the evil spirit *TSOG TSUAM* came to mind, and these men saw this evil spirit sitting on their chest, and they died, right then and there, from fright. This goes to show that emotions have a tremendous effect on our bodies, even to the point of killing us (Benson, 1997).

"Dr. Stephen Oppenheimer from Johns Hopkins University Medical School has found a small spot on the brain responsible for sudden death from fright." (Benson, 1997).

The brain is very changeable. Any time new information comes in, it totally changes from what it was previously. The brain never really reacts in the same way twice. So this means we can change the outcome of healing by thinking good thoughts, dealing with our emotions in a positive manner, and remembering healing memories.

Just think, a little sugar pill has the ability to bring about a miracle cure if it is touted as the most amazing thing ever to come across the pharmacist's counter. It was once thought the placebo effect was only 30% effective. Now new studies have shown that the placebo effect, or sugar pill effect, is 60 to 90% percent effective. "In fact, at the Scripps Clinic and Research Foundation, a study was done of asthma, herpes simplex cold sores, and duodenal ulcers using placebos. These studies concluded that in conditions of heightened expectation, sugar pills were a full 70% effective." (Benson, 1997)

"The placebo effect was again tested at the University of Washington, Seattle, and confirmed to be twice as effective as originally thought." (Benson, 1997)

Nocebo is the other side of the coin for placebo effect. If a doctor tells a person they are sick and the person believes him, then the person will start to have the symptoms of the disease. So the placebo effect can work in a negative way too (nocebo), causing all kinds of deleterious effects when a person is actually well.

Our beliefs play a major role in our health. Each and every one of us has beliefs about our health. We have beliefs about our doctor and what makes a difference in healing. If we really believe in our doctor; if we really believe in the process and what our doctor feels is the right thing to do, then we bring about a healing response based on our beliefs.

Just think of the effect medicine men had on people. In fact there have been documented cases of voodoo witch doctors pointing a finger at a person and having them drop dead from fright. Yes!

"Just thinking" we might be dying of a heart attack can cause us to die if we really believe we are. So, our beliefs have a lot to do with our healing.

What's causing all of our problems? Well, stress is the culprit. We're so stressed out… and we push all that stress down into our bodies, and there it stays.

We get stressed on the job or at home, and our unconscious makes an effort to make things right. It allows us to get sick so we don't have to go to work or get out of bed.

Plus our immune system is under attack when we are stressed. Our immune system is lowered by stress, and this allows our normal flora of bacteria and viruses to take over, making us sick. It is not just that we think we are sick. We *are* sick, with all of the aches and pains that go along with it.

If we allow ourselves to continue with large amounts of stress, years later we can end up with devastating diseases like heart disease and cancer. Most of our flu viruses, headaches, backaches, etc. are caused by stress.

In fact, the truth is that 72% to 75% of all illnesses seen by doctors are, in the words of doctors, "symptoms of today's stress." Plus, only 15 % of all diagnostic medical procedures turn up any organic cause. This translates into 54.3 billion dollars in wasted money spent on non-organic problems, that could have been treated at home with a little self-care (Benson, 1997).

Stress is estimated to cost American industry $300 billion in lost revenues from absenteeism, increased health care costs, rising insurance costs and more.

What can we do to alleviate this problem?

That's where meditation or self-hypnosis comes into play. It is just a matter of allowing ourselves to relax fully and let go of our thoughts.

I liken the mind to a computer. I mentioned this before but I will go over it again here. When we turn our computer on and we open an application, the mouse works well. But if we keep opening applications one after another, sooner or later the mouse gets stuck and we have to stop and start all over.

Well, this is what happens during the course of day-to-day events. We think we need to do this and that, and all kinds of things like take the kids to school, go to the bank, get the groceries, pick up the kids, make dinner, pay the rent, on and on and on the list goes, until our mouse (the mind) stops working and we have to stop all together.

Instead of collapsing and feeling stressed, however, we can use meditation to help us regain our center and to let our minds relax for just a few minutes.

Start by breathing in and out, perhaps doing a body scan and relaxing specific parts of your body as you work your way from your head to your toes. Then breathe in and say something to yourself that means something significant to you. Some people say a favorite prayer; some have a favorite uplifting phrase. I like to say, "I am" on the in breath, and "peaceful" on the out breath. Say this over and over again while keying in on your breathing. Sooner or later your breath will seem to disappear. If an intrusive thought comes into your mind just say "not now" to acknowledge that thought and let it flow out of your mind.

This practice will produce a sense of well being and peace throughout your whole body, if done on a daily basis.

We hold tension in our bodies chronically, producing tightness and pain. This syndrome happens when we are emotionally charged with feelings or memories and don't experience them, such as not grieving for a lost loved one. When this happens, the unconscious mind tries to keep us from the pain of the feelings and diverts our attention with bodily pain, thus creating a cycle of tension and pain. The more tension, the more pain, and the cycle never ends. This is especially true for people who don't want to deal with any emotions, never wanting to cry or get rid of the tension. They keep high on adrenaline, cortisol, and other stress-laden chemicals. These people get to the point that they don't know they are stressed. They think this is the way it is for everyone and everyone deals with emotions in the same way. No! This is not the way to deal with emotions. We have to feel them and release them from our tissues, from our brain, our mind and our soul.

Many people have compressed disks and have no pain. It is only when we have muscles contracting down that we really feel problems of lower back pain. I can attest to this fact, having been an x-ray technician. I have seen radiographs of animals and people with collapsed disks who were pain-free. It is the lack of oxygen caused by the contracted muscles that causes all the pain. When muscles contract down, oxygen can't get to tissues, and oxygen deprivation starts our pain. But the muscle contractions start by our unconscious mind providing a diversion from feeling emotions which we desperately don't want to feel.

Further, as soon as people think they have back pain they automatically stop moving, and this aggravates the pain even more. We are moving objects, and staying still aggravates the problem. The more we sit around, the more we think about our ills, the more we try not to think about emotions, the more pain and suffering we bring on ourselves. We should be doing just the opposite—keep on moving, no matter what.

The biggest thing is to acknowledge our memories and emotions. Many times repressed memories cause our pain.

Memories keep coming back and we keep not wanting to deal with them, so our unconscious mind finds a suitable diversion: "pain."Anger seems to be the biggest pain-producing emotion.

The more anger and emotions we don't confront, the more contraction and pain we feel. Contraction of muscles can cause numbness of extremities, arms, legs, and other parts of the body, while at the same time causing pain in the sciatic nerve, our joints, down our arms and legs, and just about anywhere else in our body.

Memories and emotions don't go away, they are recorded in our brains and minds forever, unless something comes along to change that. By learning something new and by looking at what has happened in the past, we can change that memory and change the brain patterns forever, and thus change the thinking that goes along with that pattern. Then we have a *new* pattern in our brain and a new way of thinking. The memory is defused, allowing our trapped bodies to relax and stopping the cycle of pain.

There is no doubt we hold on to emotions. I have a long-time friend whose grandmother died. He never grieved for his grandmother until years later when someone asked him, "How do you feel now that your grandmother is gone?" and he burst into tears, tears held back for a long, long, time.

We either express our emotions now or we express them later. Sooner or later most of us will express our pain, and until then we will feel the tension and contraction of our muscles, and deal with our emotions in a negative way.

Just expressing emotions and saying to ourselves that our unconscious thinking can no longer cause us pain, can make many back and body pains go away. I know you think that's crazy, but you know what? It works.

I had an episode that showed me just how important my unconscious thoughts and emotions are. I had been going through a time of emotional upheaval during a breakup of a long-standing relationship. I was feeling fine and laying on the couch being a couch potato, and all of a sudden my back tightened into a spasm and would not let go. I could do nothing for days and was in dire pain. Pain pills and muscles relaxants didn't do the job, but I knew just exactly what was bothering me and what I needed to do to have the pain go away. I was holding all kinds of anger, hurt and sadness about the end of the relationship that was never expressed. So I knew what I had to do: I went out into the garage and found two big two-by-two boards about four feet long and yelled and screamed and hit the floor of the garage with them, splintering the boards into a million pieces. Then I broke down into tears. I finally let out all my anger that I had bottled up inside for such a long time. Then I had a good friend who has known me for years come over and caress my head while I cried and let out all my sadness.

It was like a miraculous cure! Right away I was feeling better and two days later I was back to normal. Yes, many times pain is caused by our unconscious emotions, usually emotions we are afraid to feel and let out. We would rather be numb and in physical pain than express what we have going on inside us.

Say to yourself, "I am in conscious control of my body. I allow myself to freely express my emotions. I am pain free." Say this to yourself 30 times a day till the emotional pain is expressed and your bodily pain is gone.

Of course, people who still have problems should begin psychotherapy. This shouldn't be looked upon as bad, it is just that some people have a harder time dealing with repressed memories and need additional help to clear them. At one time or another in our lives we've all needed help, so it is fine to ask for help when we are dealing with issues from the past.

I worked with another person who had chronic neck pain for years. After finding out his pain was from anger he had never let out as a child because his mother had beat him, he set out with me to do the aforementioned daily affirmation, telling his unconscious he was in control of his life, not his unconscious. Three months later his neck pain had disappeared. Contrary to popular belief, a lot of pain is associated with emotions that have not been dealt with.

Dr. Sarno, in his book Healing Back Pain, did follow-up studies with patients with back pain. Out of 177 patients showing chronic pain, 76% are now living healthy, happy, pain-free lives. And another 8% have improved greatly from when they started going to Dr. Sarno. Another 16% were unchanged (Sarno, 1991).

What can I say? The proof is in the pudding, as the old adage goes. This method works. Our unconscious mind creates most of our pain and distracts us from the emotional issues we haven't handled.

Believing we are hurt creates pain and causes us to retire from life when we should be having the time of our lives. Our beliefs are powerful; and we shouldn't take them for granted. It is our thinking that gets in our way, not our bodies.

Again, remember always have an check up with your regular doctor to make sure there is nothing organic causing your problem. But in most cases the mind is the culprit. It is just doing its thing to keep us from feeling the pain of our emotions.

To be healthy you need a positive frame of mind. Remember that your immune system is inter-related with what you think, so think positively. Feel your emotions rather than stuffing them. Make changes in your life to deal with problems that come up. Be proactive by meditating for thirty minutes each day.

Make sure you bolster your beliefs. No matter what you believe in, it is important for your health and well being.

Write down your negative thoughts for an average day.

- _____

- _____

- _____

- _____

- _____

- _____

Look at your thoughts for the day and be honest. What negative thoughts do you have listed above? Remember, what you think and feel does make a difference in your body.

Now write down positive thoughts you might say to yourself throughout the day.

- _____

- _____

- _____

- _____

A Little More About Holding Emotions in Our Body

Many of us never think we house anything in our bodies other than flesh, blood and bone. If your day is very stressful, think about where your shoulders are in relation to your ears. Yes, they are pulled up tight. Your neck and shoulders hurt with tension you hold in your body. And what is this tension? We are always apprehensive about something happening and in so doing, this fear causes all kinds of stress. In essence, we hold emotions in our body in the same way we would hold onto a rope if we were afraid of falling.

Emotions are painful. If you have ever lost a loved one, gotten divorced, lost a job, been ill, or any of a myriad of other painful things in life, you know. In general, you try to stay away from the pains of life and hold on to the joys as much as possible.

Emotions are not released until we express them and let them out in the appropriate place and time. This means taking the time to cry and be angry. Scream at the top of your lungs, take a stick and hit a tree until you can't swing it anymore and fall down in tears. Then, and only then, will you release all that pent-up emotion that causes you so much pain and suffering within your body. Most of us become so numb to emotions that we don't even know what an emotion is, let alone how to express one. We are a society of emotionless people, for that same society says it is not right to express what we feel inside. This is where society has to change. Holding in emotions is killing the American public. It is time to change so that we might all begin to heal from the wounds of time.

As a massage practitioner, I have seen people suffer greatly because of the pent up emotions held within their bodies. Sometimes just touching certain muscles in a person's body will release an amazing amount of emotion. During a massage people have burst into tears as emotional memories are released for the first time in years. This is not fantasy, this is reality. Ask any body worker and they will tell you people hold emotions within their body.

Now, how are you going to release emotions from your body? Get in touch with who you are and what you feel. It is okay to have feelings. Feelings are not (never?) right or wrong, they are just feelings. You may choose to express your feelings by yourself or ask a very close friend if he or she would help you through this important period of time. Others may not want to be around during this expression of feelings.

Make a list of ways to express emotions you are holding inside.

- _____

- _____

- _____

- _____

- _____

Now write down a perfect time to express these feelings

- _____

- _____

- _____

Now you are on the road to healing your body through your mind. We are not separate areas of mind and body. One influences the other. We are mind/body.

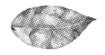

The Art of Relaxing the Mind

Meditation

The worldly-minded never come to their senses,
Even though they suffer and have terrible experiences.
Camels are very fond of thorny shrubs. The more they eat
of them, the more do their mouths bleed, yet they do not
refrain from making them their food.

—Sri Ramakrishna (Hua, 1977)

1. Does your mind race around in frenzy?
2. Do you find it hard to let go of thinking and enjoy the little things in life?
3. Do you find it hard to be in silence?
4. Do you have the radio going all the time?
5. Do you have a practice which allows you to let go of thoughts?
6. Do you have a ritual of spending time in silence during some part of the day?

Would you like to feel grounded, centered, focused, able to know your own mind, relaxed, and able to tackle what comes your way? You can find all that in meditation, a process which has been going on for thousands of years. Meditation helps people focus on what is important and let go of what is not. "In this day and age when 80% of all illnesses are somehow related to stress, we should try explore what is available to help us release our burdens and move forward toward a happier, healthier lifestyle" (Benson, 1997).

Relaxation

Many people, including myself find meditation very relaxing. It is not just for the mind, but also for the body. In fact when I meditate I can actually hear my neck relaxing. It pops and cracks as my muscles relax and let go, releasing tension that has kept my neck contracted and sometimes painful.

As you begin your meditation, be sure to breathe deeply. Scan through your whole body, relaxing every part of your being. Start with your toes and visualize a path to the top of your head. Section by section say to yourself, " I allow my toes to relax and let go," and then allow that relaxing feeling to move into your feet, and then up into your ankles until you reach the top of your head.

Finding Peace

Are you looking for peace? Calmness? Are you looking for a way to make sense of a humdrum day-in and day-out existence? These are big questions, and the only ones who seem to find answers are people who take the time each day to be very quiet. Give it a chance. You will find that many questions will be answered if you just give yourself some down time. It is when we disengage our mind that we seem to find the answers to questions. Meditation is all about letting go—so that you may find what you seek.

Spiritual Path

For those on a spiritual path, meditation is a way to become more connected with your higher calling. It offers a way to hear the higher self, a way to finally listen to what you have been hearing all along. Meditation is a part of many spiritual paths and will continue because it lets us clear our mind and that allows us to tap into our inner being. This is not the only way of connecting with our Maker, it is just another way of allowing ourselves to touch the face of God.

What is Meditation?

Webster's definition of meditation is "to reflect on; ponder. To engage in contemplation." (Simpkins, 1996) But what is meditation really? Defined from a purely scientific point of view, it is the ability to change our major brain wave patterns from Beta to Alpha or Theta.

We have to enter Alpha and Theta brain waves in order to relax enough to truly be in a meditative state.

Meditation must be experienced to truly understand what it is all about. Sometimes meditation is the emptying of thoughts from our mind and other times it is the filling of our mind with specific thoughts. No matter what, it is a balancing of the mind and body in order to promote oneness. It is a centering of all our being, so that we can put all of reality into perspective and not let any one idea or thing take over our mind and life.

Meditate to make all those crazy things you think about be put into perspective. Then you will find that only a couple of things really need your dire attention.

White Within Black, Black Within White

When you meditate you look at things a little differently. You start to see the bigger picture. You start to notice the intertwined nature of everything, how everything is like a ripple in a pond and we are part of that pond. Nothing is separate; everything is one, opposites combine to be the beginning and the end.

This is what the ancient symbol of Yin-Yang is about, the black within the white and the white within the black. Black within the white, yet one cannot live without the other, there is no black without white, there is no white without black. It is only through balance of these opposites that all elements are in harmony.

Meditation is letting go of what we have been told, what we have learned, and letting go of the self to find a greater, more effective way of being the union of opposites.

Stigmas about Meditation

The word meditation conjures up funny ideas like people sitting in the lotus position with their middle fingers and thumbs together. People get scared and think meditation is some kind of strange behavior.

But if you really think about it, daydreaming is also a type of meditation. Zoning out in front of the television or when reading a book, driving along a stretch of road and then wondering later how you got to your destination, all of these are unintentional meditations. We can also use meditation to our advantage to help us feel centered and relaxed.

History

Interestingly, the practice of meditation in other countries has been going on for thousands of years. Buddha practiced meditation under the boa tree. Saint Augustus practiced meditation during mass. He just looked at the granite floor of the cathedral and let his mind go empty in order that the presence of God might fill it. The repetitive prayers of monks are a form of meditation. Gregorian chanting is a form of meditation, some Gregorian monks chant up to eight hours a day. Even some of the rituals of the East are types of meditation such as voodoo and Sufi chanting

Meditation is practiced in many different types of disciplines such as Yoga, Chi-Qong, Tai Chi, Zen, Buddhism, Islam and more. Even self-hypnosis could be thought of as a type of specialized meditation, which allows the mind to relax and turn off and rest.

Where to Meditate

Find a nice quiet place where you can be alone. Noise can be a very big distraction and should be avoided. The area's temperature should be comfortable, and you should have a nice comfortable place to sit. You could lie down, but most people have a tendency to fall asleep. Make sure the room is relatively warm. If you're cold, it is hard to relax.

Some people like to use an "asana" or a woolen blanket or mat to sit on. Still others like to use a round meditation pillow to sit on (Sivananda Yoga Vedanta Center, 1993). My personal preference is to use one pillow behind me as I lean against something and another under my buttocks to allow pressure to be taken off my knees while I sit cross-legged. This seems to be the most comfortable for me. You can even sit in a straight-backed chair. It is most important to be comfortable and erect so you can breathe.

How Long Should I Meditate?

This depends on the individual, but many famous gurus and teachers recommend at least 30 minutes a day. Still others like to meditate for as long as an hour. Monks, Gurus, holy ones may even meditate for weeks. Most people I know who meditate for extended periods of time are very good at meditation but not very good at life. I recommend 30 minutes a day. Meditation is to help you deal with life, not become your life.

Start out with five minutes and slowly work your way up to 30 minutes. If you are worried about losing track of time set a timer to go off at the end of your meditation. Then you won't have to worry about being late for work or some pressing appointment.

Breath Work

Our breath is very important and is an integral part of all types of meditative disciplines. Breathing is something we do automatically. Even if we hold our breath, eventually we will pass out and start breathing again. So it is something we have control over, and at the same time do not have control over. This makes it perfect to key in on when we meditate. During meditation as we key in on our breathing, our breathing seems to disappear as if it weren't there. This is because it is such an automatic part of our being that

122

we don't have to think about it at all. That is why our breath is the perfect mechanism to key on for meditation.

Our breath is also the key to energizing our body. As we breathe we take in oxygen that allows us to burn our food and create energy, or life force. This life force is called many different names such as *"Chi"* in Chinese or *"Prana"* in Sanskrit.

Music

Some people like to meditate to music and others like silence. Whichever you choose, just make sure the music doesn't take over your mind. Listen to something non-repetitive and with no distinctive beat. An exception to that is the distinctive beat of native drumming. Native drums seem to carry us far away from our busy mind and allow us to escape for awhile. No one is really sure why this works the way it does. My personal feeling is that native drumming puts you into a hypnotic state which is very relaxing.

Clothing

Wear loose-fitting clothing with bare feet or socks, or very comfortable shoes or slippers. Restrictive clothing will take your attention away from meditation.

When to Meditate

You can meditate anytime, but finding a particular time every day is best. I once had a client who was a Zen meditator; he would meditate every day at noon. He was a writer and would get up in the morning and start writing. Soon he would get frantic thinking about all the deadlines that were coming up and nothing would get accomplished. Then at noon he would meditate and the rest of the day would go more smoothly. He came to me asking what to do to deepen his meditation practice so his whole day would go better. I replied that when you write you need a piece of paper to write on. Meditation is the paper you write your life on—start with the paper. So he started meditating every day first thing in the morning and from then on his days went smoothly.

Find a time that works for you. I recommend meditating early in the morning. I also find that meditating two or three times a day keeps me centered. Also, meditating just before sleep helps me sleep very deeply.

Posture

Posture is very important. If you are in a very uncomfortable position you won't be able to keep that position for very long. If you sit upright with crossed legs or in an upright chair, you will find it much easier to sit for an extended period of time. Keep your spine as straight as possible but don't force a posture, make it easy and relaxed. Many people find keeping their hands on their legs comfortable, one hand on each leg so their hands are not touching each other.

Clasped hands can sometimes be a distraction because of the sensory input from our hands to one another. For others clasped hands feel comfortable and natural.

I particularly like to have a pillow behind me so I can lean against something with my back, but that's my personal preference. The most important thing is relaxing and letting go of tension in your body. If you are not relaxed because of your position, you really need to find out what position will work for you.

I know when I first started meditating the thought of having a straight spine made me feel uncomfortable, but after the first five or six minutes I was able to relax and let go and meditate.

Body Awareness

During meditation our mind can become very aware of our body. Have you ever noticed that your shoulders are up around your ears, signaling that you need to relax and let your shoulders down? Well, when we sit for an extended period of time and allow ourselves to just *be*, we finally key in on what tension we have going on in our body. During the hustle and bustle of each day we forget to key in on what we are feeling in our bodies until it all builds up and causes some kind of problem. Through meditation, we can notice all the little things that are going on with our body, what tensions we feel, and relax those areas causing us pain.

We notice places that need our attention and use this feedback to help our body heal. Perhaps through exercise, good quality food, relaxation, vitamins, stretching, massage, yoga, and other modalities we can help our body to become the body we want.

Eyes Open or Closed

Having your eyes open or closed is a personal preference, it really doesn't matter. I think most people meditate with their eyes closed because it is easier to let go of distractions that way. If you are a visual person, sometimes visual images can cause your mind to create thoughts and make it difficult to clear thoughts from your mind.

For others it works very well to just look at an interesting or tranquil scene and let go of thinking. You could look down and just gaze at a plain floor or look at a plain wall. It doesn't matter. In Zen meditation one is to look at nothingness such as a plain wall, until all of a sudden your mind is freed from its boundaries and you fly away in your meditation.

Attitude

One must adopt an open attitude to meditate and be willing to let go of being in control. This can be very frightening for people who find it very hard to let go of always having things as they like them. You have to let go of anticipating or expecting things to happen, for in meditation you never know what is going to happen. Meditation is all about letting the computer/mind rest for a little while, until it regroups and restores itself.

If you always have to be in control, meditation is definitely not for you. But if you are looking for a way to stop trying to be the ruler of the universe and let go of control, I highly recommend meditation.

Of course there are times when a meditation can seem to have a specific purpose in mind, so even if your mind wanders, go with it.

Don't try to force it. Let go, it might be important. But on the average, the mind just needs a little training to focus on nothing and just *be* for a while.

Sometimes during the course of your regular meditation feelings will come up, but if you are a control freak this won't happen. Emotions come up for a reason, they are trying to get your attention, and when you finally relax for the first time, all of a sudden they may come welling up to the surface. Don't be alarmed, just go with the flow, feel the feelings and let them out. Let the tears flow, let the sadness out, feel the joy; whatever it is, feel it and know it is all part of being human. For even Jesus and Buddha had feelings and felt joy and sadness. Why should you be any different about letting go of control and feeling?

Open Mindedness

During a meditation it is best to drop any and all preconceived judgements. Stop all analytical thinking and let go of the way you think things *should* be. By doing this you open yourself up to all kinds of discoveries about yourself, about everything and everyone around you. But if you have judgements about things, you have   already closed the door on learning anything new. So try to be open-minded, let thoughts run in and out and just let them *be*, let the images play and don't judge what is happening

Types of Meditation

It is believed there are two major groups of meditation, one is yang or active meditation and the other is yin or passive meditation. Yang meditation is actively trying to do something with your mind. Yin is just letting go of the thoughts and worries of the physical world.

There are many different types of meditation from *Yoga* styles to *Zen* Buddhist. Most forms of meditation tend to use breath work to help center the mind and body. In yoga the breath is call *prana* and in Buddhism it is called *chi*, the life force or energy of the mind/body.

A General Over View Of Yoga Meditation

That which frees one from sorrow
and brings real bliss is Yoga.
—Swami Chidananda (Hua, 1977)

"In yoga the breath is concentrated on and linked to the pulse in order to achieve the special desired effects. Using special postures and visualization can allow prana to be absorbed and stored within the body to help heal."(Simpkins, 1996). The stored energy is concentrated in special centers of the body called *chakras*. It is kind of like recharging a battery. Life force is used every day, so to rejuvenate, more life force is brought in and stored away for healing.

Placing the body in a straight posture, with the
chest, throat and head held erect, making the
organs together with the mind perfectly
established in the lotus of the heart, the sage
crosses all the fearful currents of ignorance
by means of the raft of Brahman.

— The Upanishads

The yogis withdraw their minds from the distractions of the outside world so they can be free to achieve higher consciousness or enlightenment. The practice of yoga promotes health, cleanliness, good diet, and a long life.

Raja Yoga

In Raja Yoga direct training and control of the mind is all important in order to achieve enlightenment. Focused attention, perception, and intense concentration help clear the mind of all extraneous thoughts.

Gnani Yoga

In Gnani Yoga wisdom is the path to enlightenment using philosophical study and concentration on insights to achieve oneness with the universe.

Bhakti Yoga

Bhakti Yoga focuses on the Love of God in order to find enlightenment. Bhakti yogis tend to laugh, sing, be loving, optimistic, positive and cheerful. Jesus, Buddha, Muhammad and Mother Teresa are all of this persuasion. This yoga is very much the yoga of selfless devotion to others.

Karma Yoga

Karma Yoga is a specialized yoga dealing with work. Karma's root word comes from the letters KR and means " to effect" or to make a change in something. This yoga wishes to make the effect of work a positive experience. It is not the outcome but the process that is important in Karma Yoga. Suffering is looked upon as part of the process and is not avoided but accepted as part of the scheme of things. Work is a meditative effort and through work nirvana is achieved.

Mantra Yoga

Mantra Yoga is another specialized yoga in which a word or syllable is used to chant and focus on in order that the conscious mind might have something to keep it busy. Thus the unconscious mind is opened up and allowed to be free. Also in this trance state there is the ability to let go of everything around us and become centered within one's self. A person practicing Mantra Yoga silently concentrates on a word he or she had chosen. Yogis believe concentration on a mantra can lead to enlightenment.

Kundalini Yoga

"Kundalini is a specialized type of yoga for revitalizing the vital force that lies dormant in all of us, leading toward spiritual enlightenment and salvation using Mantras, specialized asanas for the body, and visualization to move vital energy from one chakra to another, eliminating energy blocks" (Legion, 1999).

Vipassana or Mindfulness Meditation

The word *vipassana* come from Sanskrit and means "insight." Many different traditions have mindfulness meditation techniques. Mindfulness is a way of being in the Buddhist tradition, a way of being fully here-and-now in every moment we are alive. Being fully alive and aware is something most of us never experience, we take this moment for granted by letting it slip away into the past without ever savoring its beauty.

Mindfulness meditation and training is letting go of the past, letting go of the future, and being in the present. This training is wonderful for people who are so future-oriented and driven to produce that they forget to enjoy life. Life is not a series of doings; it is being that is important. Another way of putting it is, "it is about being happy" not "doing happy." Many people can't sit still for a single second; they always have to be accomplishing something. Sooner or later these people end up in the coronary care section of a hospital or the chemotherapy area of a cancer ward. We are not built to push ourselves all the time. We were made to enjoy life. We are not here to make money so others can enjoy life after we are dead

Thich Nhat Hanh tells of "washing dishes, just to wash the dishes." How many of us do that? Most of the time we are washing dishes to get to some other function, or thinking about something we have to get done after we wash the dishes. We are so removed from the moment that we lose it altogether.

Happiness is being in the moment and enjoying the moment. This is one of the major effects of meditation, it keeps us in the moment. Just think about what you are doing right now; you are probably sitting down enjoying reading this. What is there to worry about? Nothing! In this moment all is well. But we forget and start to worry about the future. We transport ourselves to a possibility of a future that might not even occur. The past is over and done with and who knows what the future will be like; be *here* right now! Mindfulness doesn't require any specific knowledge. You don't have to study mindfulness, you just have to experience being totally present and in the moment, enjoying this very second.

"Mindfulness must be engaged." This means being mindful at all times, living a meditation, noticing all the little things that go on around you, and being at peace with the world (Thich Nhat Hanh, 1991).

John Kabat-Zin teaches mindfulness training at his center in Massachusetts (Kabat-Zinn, 1996). Doctors from all over the country send heart and cancer patients to his center to learn to live mindfully. And Thich Nhat Hanh teaches mindfulness meditation at Plum Village, a Buddhist village nestled in the heart of France.

Zen Meditation

Zen in Japanese means "*meditation*." "Zen is the experience of the higher truth and reality through direct transmission of insight from mind to mind, irrespective of doctrines, temples, organizations, and rituals" (Simpkins, 1996). Comprehension does not come from analysis but it does come from solving a puzzle. "Zen is realizing what simply is" (Simpkins, 1996). Enlightenment occurs by grace, not logic. This grace may happen after years of study or out of the blue at any time. Grace is accepting what is and what is not, allowing everything to be as will be. Grace is opening ourselves up to all possibilities.

Zen is doing nothing and thinking nothing, it is just being. "Even a good thing is not so good as nothing" is a Zen phrase (Simpkins, 1996).

Zen meditation is about emptying the mind and doing nothing. For instance, after sitting and looking at a blank wall for an hour, all of a sudden the wall starts to change and have colors, and you have visions of things you have no idea about.

Zen Buddhist temples are everywhere, and a story was related to me of people who spend time in a temple learning to let go of "the self" or " mind" and being free. During a week's stay no words are spoken, and only hand gestures are used to communicate such things as "this is enough food". They meet every day in the main hall and meditate for hours. Not a word is spoken and if you start to fall asleep, a temple priest comes by with a bamboo stick and first taps you on the shoulder and then raps you hard with the stick.

During the first couple of days you get very tired of sitting in one position and not moving; it seems unbearable at times. But after a couple of days, that unbearable feeling drops away.

At first it is very hard trying to meditate for such a long time. But soon everything starts to drop away and all of a sudden you get angry for having to put up with all of the nonsense. But you can do nothing and have to stay in control.

A couple of days later the anger subsides and you started to weep and cry uncontrollably about everything and nothing. But you can not wipe your tears, nose, or anything, so your nose drips and tears roll down your face. At first you want to do something, but if you move you will get rapped again by the stick. After awhile it just didn't matter anymore and you let your nose and tears flow— and flow they do. Everything you experienced as being human is being washed away and you are reducing down to your essence. All of your ego, your materialism, your needs, and wants are washed away until you are a puddle sitting in one spot in the temple.

Next comes a feeling of calm and peacefulness inside and the feeling that you don't want to *stop* being silent and forced to sit still for such long periods of time. In fact you start to love being hit by the priest with the stick for it is the only contact you have and a feeling of being loved invades your whole being every time you are hit. It is amazing what nothingness will do to a person; sometimes it can help a person find out who they really are deep down inside.

Taoism

Taoism is a philosophy and type of meditation that reflects the thinking of the great philosopher Lao-Tzu of 604 BC. Taoism is basically the law of no effort, that there is nothing to oppose. There is a union of opposites; one is in the other so there are no opposites, as in the yin-yang symbol. Taoism teaches people to find their true nature and listen to it. Like driving a car on ice, if the car is turned into a spin the car straightens out. And from this, it can be said that life straightens out if we use the flow of life to our advantage.

The practice of taoism seeks to bring out the good in all of us. Everyone has a tendency to be in balance. "Going with the flow" comes from the Tao principle. No action is to be contrary to nature.

"Who can find repose in a muddy world
— By lying still, it becomes clear."
—Tao te Ching

The nature of Tao is –
Looked at, but cannot be seen—
That is called the invisible
Listened to but cannot be heard—
That is called the inaudible
Grasped at, but cannot be touched—
That is called the Intangible
These three elude all our inquiries
And hence blend and become one.
—Tao te Ching

Concentration Meditation

Concentrating on something is another way of meditating. Just gazing at a candle, concentrating on it deeply and watching the flame, is an example. You can use just about anything, a rock, or the ocean, or even a written page of scripture. All that is important is that you put your full attention on whatever you are looking at.

Some people find after awhile what they are looking at seems to transmute and change. Another way of putting it is that the mind is freed from its boundaries and is free to produce whatever it wants in our unconscious and conscious mind. Sometimes objects will change in color, shape, size, whatever the mind sees will happen. The most important thing is not to judge what is going on. This allows a feeling of oneness, relaxation and peace to start growing, allowing you to let go of your worries.

Give this meditation method a try and write down what your experience was like below.

- _____

- _____

- _____

Self-Hypnosis or Creative Visualization

Self-hypnosis or creative visualization is also another way to meditate. Most people don't think of it this way, but in actuality hypnosis, prayer, being still, being in nature, mantras, or anything else which induces a semi-trance state is meditation. This occurs any time we meditate, start to touch parts of us that are elusive to us in our normal waking state. It is said by some that meditation, prayer, or the act of being quiet, is to touch the face of God. Others say to meditate or to be still is to come into contact with the God-like part of ourselves.

The Rose Technique for Self-Hypnosis

This technique was covered earlier. Go back and review that section (page 87) to remind you just how simple this techniques is and how it can be used as a meditation practice.

Try the rose technique. Where you able to relax and let your mind go for awhile? Write down your experience below.

- _____

- _____

- _____

Breath Work Meditation

My particular brand of meditation is every easy to use and understand. Just get comfortable and sit with an erect position. Sitting upright is easier for long periods of time and more comfortable. You may sit cross-legged, or in the lotus position if you prefer, but it is not necessary. Just sitting in a nice upright chair is fine. Place your hands in a comfortable position in your lap and allow yourself to close your eyes, or you can just cast your gaze downward.

Take a nice deep breath and start to key in on your breathing. Notice your breath coming into your nose and on down into the deepest part of your lungs. Then notice your breath as it leaves and starts from the bottom of your lungs and works its way out to the tip of your nose. Just keep focusing all your attention on your breathing.

Whenever a thought enters your mind, just acknowledge it and say to yourself, "I see that, but not now" and let it pass on out of your mind. But it is important to acknowledge each thought; otherwise it will keep coming back and interrupting your meditation. Then by saying to yourself, "I see that, but not now," and letting it flow out of your head, you can go back to concentrating on your breath. And you may do this whole process over and over again. When you are ready, take a deep breath and come back to the room.

Try breath work meditation. Breath work is used in many different types of meditation.

Write down your experience with breath work meditation below.

- _____

- _____

- _____

Are You Falling Asleep During Meditation?

Sometimes you may feel like falling asleep. One way to get around this feeling is to imagine yourself sitting on the edge of a deep well. Whenever you start to fall asleep you will automatically wake up trying not to fall in the well.

Have An Itch?

If you have an itch or need to move, by all means move. It is just easier to make one little move than to be in agony throughout the whole meditation. But on the other hand, after awhile the body will become secondary to stilling the mind, and the need to itch or stretch will go away.

A Zen student went to his meditation teacher saying, "My meditation is terrible! I'm so distracted, or my legs hurt, or I'm constantly falling asleep. It's just horrible!" "It will pass," the teacher said matter-of-factly. A week later, the student came back to his teacher. "My meditation is great! I feel so aware, so peaceful, so alive! It's just wonderful!" "It will pass," the teacher replied matter-of-factly.

Our Inner Song

"In Africa when a woman decides to conceive a child she goes out into a field so she can find the child's song. She sits there until she can clearly hear the song of the new child and starts to sing the song. Then she sings the song all the way back to the village and back to her home. She and her spouse sing the song as they conceive the baby. Then the mother sings the song throughout the pregnancy. During the birth the whole village gathers round and sings the song to the baby.

Throughout the life of the child whenever a lesson is learned, the village people sing the song. When something happens to the child again they sing their song.

When the child becomes an adult, finds a mate and marries again the song is sung. This goes on throughout his or her whole life until at the very end of their life, again their song is sung for the last time"(Kornfield, 1972).

Perhaps meditation is like finding our song, so listen carefully to the silence, you might find your song, a song to sing throughout your whole life. Find a song within your heart that will help you travel the road of life.

Practice

"...meditation is very much like training a puppy. You put the puppy down and say, "Stay." Does the puppy listen? It gets up and it runs away. You set the puppy back down again. "Stay." And the puppy runs away over and over again. Sometimes the puppy jumps up, runs over, and pees in the corner or makes some other mess. Our minds are much the same as the puppy's, only they create even bigger messes. In training the mind, or the puppy, we have to start over and over again" (Jack Kornfield, 1972).

Another way you can think of the mind is as the "monkey mind." A monkey jumps from this to that and back again, and that is just exactly how the human mind works, jumping from one thing to another. So we have to appease the "monkey," training it to sit still for just a little while so we can let go of thoughts. Start out with just one minute a day, then two minutes, then four, and then eight, on up to fifteen and finally to thirty minutes. Within that thirty minutes of sitting you will still find all kinds of treasures of the heart, soul and mind, while the body relaxes and lets go of tension (Hahn, 1977).

Sleep is Not the Same Thing

I know what you're thinking. I already sleep seven to nine hours a day, so what's the difference? I let go of thinking then!

You think you do! But in reality we dream, and these dreams are just as psycho-active as being out in the real world. So you need to let go of dreams, let go of thinking, and just *be* for a little while. In fact a person can wake up feeling even more tired than at bedtime. Many times muscle tension never goes away during sleep. This means we really need to meditate to let the body relax and just *be* for a while.

When we dream we go through the same stress changes as when we are awake, it just depends on what we are dreaming. It might be relaxing or stressful. If you dream of running away from a lion, your adrenaline level goes up, as does your heart rate and your blood pressure as well. Now, that's not a relaxing dream.

Love Meditation

One of my favorite meditations is the Love meditation. Let yourself get comfortable, take a couple of deep breaths, and let go of all muscle tension. Allow your toes to relax, then your feet, and on up into your ankles. Now allow your calves to relax and let this feeling slowly move into your knees and on up into your legs, letting them feel loose and lazy. Allow your abdomen to relax and all your internal organs. Focus on feeling soothed. Allow your heart to relax and your lungs. Let all those muscles in your back go heavy and let all your weight sink on down.

Let your shoulders droop and allow this relaxing feeling to move on down your upper arms through your lower arms, then on down your wrists and hands and out through your fingertips. Allow your throat to relax and the back of your neck, then up the back of your head and over the top of your head, soothing and relaxing your forehead, letting all those little lines flatten out. Relax your eyes and eyelids, including all those muscles around your eyes. Allow your face to relax, your nose, your cheeks, your jaw, and let your teeth separate just a little. Allow your lips to relax, and the sides of your face, and your ears.

Now imagine a beautiful white light coming down from the heavens and touching the top of your head, filling your whole head with warming, healing light from above. Allow that light of love to come down into your body, healing as it fills your whole body.

Notice the light growing brighter around your heart. See it grow brighter and brighter until it bursts forth and pours all around your body, healing everything it touches. This light covers every inch of your body, enveloping your whole being in this healing light of love.

Then this light starts to grow. First it is the size of your body, and then it is twice the size of your body. Then it fills the room, and then the building. Feel the light expand to fill a city block, then a few blocks, and on out to include the city. Then this light of love expands ever wider to take in the county, and then the state, expanding to the size of the country.

This healing light of love expands to take in North America, then on to include the continent, and then the world. Then this healing light of love expands even more from your heart, reaching to the moon, the planets, and on out to take in the whole galaxy, and then all the galaxies and finally the Universe where you reach out to touch the face of God, the Creator, The Alpha and Omega, The Beginning and the End.

Now this love comes back to you, back to the galaxies, back to the planets, back to the world, back to the continent, and back to the country. The healing light of love comes back to the county, the city, the few blocks and on back to your building, and back to your room, then half of the room, back to twice the size of your body, and back to your heart. You have filled your heart with the healing light of Universal love and compassion for yourself and everyone else. This healing light of love that will glow on forever within your heart.

Try this technique and allow yourself to open up and let love in. Write down your experience below.

- _____

- _____

- _____

Forgiveness Meditation

One of the most remarkable meditations is the forgiveness meditation. We all have known people who have made us angry or have wronged us. If we hold onto hate and anger, they will have negative effects on our mind and body.

My father was a person who was very angry with his family for disowning him and his new wife from the family because he had married out of their religious faith. His family eventually forgot the whole thing and wanted to get to know my mom. But my dad wouldn't let go and held onto his anger forever.

If not released, these types of emotions will be carried in the body. My dad started to have arthritis, and ended up with arthritic wrists, knees and fingers. He kept carrying this anger around with him that he wouldn't release, and it came out in his body in the form of arthritis.

Jack Kornfield tells a story of two men who were held captive in a war camp for years. Once the war was over they met at a party and one of the men came up to the other and asked, "Have you forgiven the people who imprisoned you?" And the other man answered, "Never. I'll never forgive them for what they did to me until the day I die." And the first man answered, "Well, then, they still have you in prison, don't they? (Kornfield, Video).

To start this meditation take a nice long breath and allow your eyes to close, breath deeply, and let all that tension just flow away. Now imagine a healing light from the heavens coming in again and filling your whole being, expanding until it bursts, from your heart like a giant searchlight.

Now imagine someone who has wronged you, someone with whom you are angry, someone you possibly hate. Perhaps someone from the past, living or not, it doesn't matter. See this person standing in front of you and notice his body seems translucent and made of a dark black cloudy mist.

Stand face to face with this person and notice this mist coming up through his body and beginning to concentrate at his heart, then bursting out of his heart and moving toward you. Feel your own heart full of the healing light of love coming out to meet this dark black cloud of mist. And when the two columns meet in the middle, see that the light burns away all the black mist. Watch it burning away all the blackness, burning away all the darkness, and burning away the cloud. Burning away the cloud to the point where your healing light of heavenly love fills his heart with love as well.

See that healing light fill his heart and grow beyond the borders of the heart to include all of the chest, then the abdomen, then down into his legs and feet. Then your healing light fills his arms, his neck and flows up into his head, illuminating every cell in his body.

This healing light of love from the heavens expands to twice the size of the other person to include you. It is a soothing, loving light of love. Then you walk even closer and the two of you melt into each other's arms and step into each other's bodies and become one. Now you know what the other person is feeling, all the sadness, all the fear, all his feelings of not being worthy. Now you discover all the feelings you never saw when you looked at him before. You stay in this embrace for a little while, then separate again, knowing you both are fine. Take a few deep breaths and slowly come back to the room.

I was once giving a meditation workshop and had just finished the love and forgiveness meditations in that order, when a woman from the audience came up to me and said she had just forgiven someone from her past whom she had not been able to forgive for years.

Give these two meditations a try. You may be surprised by what might happen. Write down your experience below.

- _____

- _____

Candle Meditation

Another way to meditate is to gaze deeply into a candle. For as long as people have been around fire, people have been mesmerized by the dance of the flame. Have you ever looked at the fire burning in your fireplace and been entranced by its hypnotic character? Of course you have, we all have. This is the same feeling that has been going down through time, for as long as men have been able to observe fire.

Light a candle in front of you and get comfortable. Look deeply into the flame. Take a deep breath and let go of any body tension. Take another deep breath and let go of feelings and ideas that no longer serve you.

Now gaze deep within the candle and look at the different parts of the flame. See the wick, and the little area of glowing red that surrounds the tip of the wick. Now look at the blue glow at the bottom of the flame. Then the green flame just above the blue color. Look at the white light from the center of the flame and then on to the yellow-orange color at the tip of the flame. The glow around the candle and the smoke from the very tip, all parts together yet distinctly different.

As you gaze at this flame allow thoughts to come in and say to yourself, "I see that, but not now," and continue gazing deep within the candle. The candle is a living, breathing thing. It takes in oxygen and burns wax to create energy, in a way similar to taking in food. We are very similar to the candle, for we have many parts that make up who we are, and yet we are one whole, like the candle.

The wick is the divine energy of love that was breathed into us from long ago, animating us and giving us life. The glow at the tip of the wick is the spark of our soul, our spirit, which keeps our life light burning. The blue light at the base of the flame is our base chakra, grounding us to this world of reality. The green light is our spirit of the second chakra, or the sexual chakra, our creativity, our expression of making our passage in the world. The white light is our third chakra, our solar plexus, our drive, our way of protecting ourselves, our gut feeling that helps us do what we intuitively know is right.

The yellow light is our fourth chakra, or our heart chakra, our center for love, our way of being compassionate, our ability to be vulnerable and open to love. The orange light is our fifth chakra, or our throat chakra, our ability to speak, to put into words what we want from life, our intention, our desires, our ability to ask for what we need. The glow around the candle is our sixth chakra, or our third eye chakra, our inner vision, our ability to see from within, to see what might be, to see all possibilities the future might hold.

The smoke at the tip of the candle is the seventh chakra, or the crown chakra, our wisdom, our ability to deduce, our innate ability to know, our inner knowledge, our ability to take knowledge and combine it with wisdom.

The candle itself is the eighth chakra, our whole being, and our combined matrix of mind, body, and spirit, separate yet all one indivisible crystalline structure, vibrating at such a high frequency that we become physical matter, our aura, our soul.

Now take another couple of breaths and come on back to the room.

Could you see the candle in your mind's eye? Write down your experience below.

- _____

- _____

Mindfulness Meditation

One meditation I like to use for mindfulness is meditating on a simple object. It can be anything from an apple to a zuccihni, it doesn't matter what it is, but I like to use food. Most of us never think about grapes, we just grab a handful and gulp them down. Let's look at a grape in a different way.

Sit comfortably and pull out a bunch of grapes. Breathing deeply, take one grape from the bunch and hold it in your fingers. Look closely at the grape. Notice the texture of the grape. Notice the color, what color would you say it is? Notice the sheen of the grape. How big is the grape? Feel the texture of the grape in your fingers. Is it hard, soft, mushy? Notice any little color changes in the skin of the grape. Notice where the stem used to be. Notice how the grape comes together to attach to the stem. Notice how the light plays on the surface of the grape.

Take a deep breath and take a small bite of the grape. How did it feel? What does it taste like? What does it feel like on your tongue? What areas of your mouth does it affect? Where do you taste it in your mouth? What does it smell like?

Take a deep breath and look at the piece of grape still in your hands. What does the inside of the grape look like? What color is it? Does it have a different texture? How does the light play on the inside of the grape? Squeeze the grape in your fingers and notice how the insides squish out.

Look at this grape over a period of an hour. It may be hard to do this, but in the end you will have a deeper appreciation of a grape. As well as a greater understanding of your ability to see and take in the beauty around you.

Now take this practice into your home. Eat dinner mindfully by noticing all the colors, texture, aromas, and tastes as you slowly eat your meal. This is a way of slowing down your life and appreciating all the little treasures around you. All of life can become a ritual. All of your daily tasks can become a ritual. All can be beautiful and spiritually significant.

Every single thing you do throughout your day can become a mindful experience. Through the process of being mindful you will become more connected with your daily life, your environment, and your inner spirit.

Look at pleasant scene in the woods for a very long time. Notice all the little things that go on. Notice the light change as the sun moves across the sky. Notice the insects as they crawl on the ground or fly by. Take in the birds as they soar through the sky, the squirrel as he scurries up a tree, and the leaves as they sway in the wind. Notice everything you've missed before. Then breathe deeply, taking in everything around you. This is a great way to slow down and take in life. This technique is used by many hospitals to teach post-surgery coronary patients to slow down and smell the roses.

Were you able to sit for a full hour totally in tune with the grape? Write down your experience below.

- _____

- _____

- _____

- _____

Driving Meditation

Do you drive a lot? Are you in the car for hours at a time? Then why not try this. Concentrate totally on your driving, concentrate on what you're doing in the car, how the wheel is turning, where you're going, the road, and what other cars are doing as you drive along. When an extraneous thought comes into your head just say to yourself "I see that, but not right now," and go back to concentrating on driving. You will be safer because you're concentrating on driving, let alone the benefits of letting go of extraneous thoughts that get in the way of being in the moment. A wandering mind keeps us in the future or the past and we miss out on this special moment happening right now. When we are totally in the moment we are fully alive and totally present to enjoy the gift of this very second. Give it a try, you'll find it refreshing and delightful.

150

Healing Meditation

A healing meditation can be used for yourself or others. Imagine yourself or someone else sitting back and relaxing. Starting at the tips of your toes and moving all the way up to the top of your head, allow all those areas of your body to relax. Take a couple of deep breaths and let go of even more stress. We all deserve to relax and let go, and to feel safe and warm and always in control.

Now imagine a color wheel in front of you, whirling around and stopping at the most healing color at the top of the wheel. Then notice another color wheel with the same healing color, but with different shades. See it whirling around in front of you and when it stops, the most healing shade of the color will be at the top of the wheel.

Just let go and imagine yourself looking in a mirror, see yourself standing there, see your body from the inside out. See an outline of your body, and your body full of colors from head to toe. Notice the colors of your body in areas that are bothering you. What color are they? What shades of color are they? Then imagine your healing color coming in and healing that area of your body. The original color slowly fades away and your healing color slowly takes over, feel it healing, soothing, and changing all the ill effects of that old color until the old color is totally gone.

Notice your whole body filled with that healing color from head to toe. Notice how good your body feels, how soothed your body is, how relaxed your whole body feels, and how great it is to feel that healing in your body.

When you're ready, take a couple of deep breaths and slowly come back to the room.

This meditation can help you connect with your mind/body, increasing healing and relaxing you at the same time. What did you experience during this meditation?

- _____

- _____

- _____

Meditation for Sports

Meditation can be used for very practical aspects of life. My brother flies for a major airline which encourages pilots to visualize takeoffs and landings just before actually getting in the plane.

Meditation is used by many different people for many different reasons each day depending on the circumstances, but most of the time they don't see it as meditation. Visualizations are also another way of meditating.

Athletes will visualize a particular aspect of a sport at which they want to excel. Through this visualization they can see themselves swinging the golf club in a perfect swing, or swimming the best free-style race ever, or playing the best round of tennis they could imagine.

Athletes can apply this to particular problems they having. Perhaps they are having a batting problem, so they visualize batting the correct way until they can feel the bat in their hands. If you have a problem breaking your golf swing, visualize yourself swinging in slow motion, see what's causing the problem, then see yourself swinging through in slow motion with the correct golf swing. See this swing in your mind over and over again until you have it memorized. Variations on this technique can be used for any aspect of any sport. Adapt your meditation to fit what it is you are trying to improve.

If you're into sports, give this meditation a try and write your feelings below after the exercise.

- _____

- _____

- _____

- _____

Meditation for Changing Your Life

Do you know what you want in life? Can you close your eyes and see it in your mind's eye? How are you going to create what you want if you can't see it? Sit down and think about all the details right down to where, when, and with whom. See yourself doing just what you want to do! Look at the image just before this image, and the one just after. Take it all in, and run it over and over again in your mind, until you know it by heart.

Write down a list of steps you need to take in order to make this happen. Set a realistic schedule, one you can use to finish all these steps. As you work through each one mark it off and move on to the next one. In no time you will achieve your dream. It all starts with a seed within your mind, for without the vision there can be no fruition.

We all need to change something in our lives—give it a try and write down your experience below.

- _____

- _____

- _____

Meditation for Solving with Problems

Sit comfortably and let go of all stress and all tension in your body. Scan your body from head to toe, relaxing every part of your body as you go.

Think of yourself in a very wonderful place, perhaps somewhere you have been before, or an imaginary place. Just choose a relaxing, soothing, peaceful place to be, and let go of all the tension in your body.

Now keep that wonderful place in mind and concentrate on your problem. Think of all the possible parts to the puzzle, all the people involved, and all possible ways of dealing with it. Think of all the intricate details that make up this problem.

Think of all the ways it might turn out, and the ways this problem could affect your life and the lives of others. Think of your judgements, be they positive or negative, as just bits of knowledge and let them go.

Then go back to your wonderful place and let go of all thinking about this problem. Say to yourself, "I let go of all thoughts on this subject. I am free of attachment to this problem." Then let go of all thinking about your problem and go back to your wonderful place once again.

Detach yourself from the problem by saying, "I don't care, it will all work one way or another and I don't care. I am open to new avenues and directions for the future."

Stay here for a few moments and then slowly come back to the room. You may find the answers to your problem may come right away, or in hours, or perhaps days, but sooner or later the answer will come to you. Letting go of problems allows your unconscious mind to find answers previously beyond reach. It is in the void of not thinking and worrying that our unconscious mind can be very creative and find answers to problems.

We all have something that is a problem in our life and we all could use some help solving problems. Give this meditation a try and see how it can make a difference in your life. List some problems you want to work on below.

- _____

- _____

Awareness Meditation

Another way to meditate is to name everything that comes into your awareness physically and mentally during your meditation. For instance, if you have an itch, notice the itch and acknowledge the itch. Once you have given it attention and awareness of its existence, sooner or later the itch will disappear on its own. If you have a feeling such as anger coming up, say to yourself silently or out loud, "anger," and let it go and soon it will pass. Later you may have sadness come up; say to yourself "sadness" and let it pass.

Take the time to do this meditation. It is a wonderful way to key in on everything going on in your mind and body.

Checking in with ourselves is very important and can bring us great insight as to what we're feeling and what's happening in our life. What did you discover during this meditation? Write it down below.

- _____

- _____

- _____

Meditation for Relationships

Do you have someone in your life who is a problem or someone you don't get along with? You may want to try this meditation for relationships.

When we look at a relationship we can only look at ourselves because we are the only ones we can change. People all around you are perfect just the way they are, and it is up to us to make our relationships work.

Anger, hate, judgment and lots of other emotions get in the way of having a harmonious relationship and cloud the waters of harmony. Our negative emotions keep us judging and never let us see the truly wonderful qualities of the other person. It is only when we let all the muddy waters from our own inner being settle that we are finally able to have a wonderful relationship.

This meditation is about changing you and not the other person, though it allows you to send positive healing energy to them so they can understand us better.

Relax and let go of tension in your body, scanning your whole body from head to toe, relaxing each area of your body as you go. Take a couple of deep breaths and let go of even more tension, for your breath is your own built-in natural tranquilizer.

Now imagine anyone about whom you want to meditate is standing in front of you. This can include you! Say silently, "I forgive you for what you have done to me, and you forgive me for what I have done to you, and I forgive myself." See in your mind's eye a healing golden rain of light from your Higher Power, your Creator, your God.

Now in your mind say to that person, "I love you and just want you to become more of who you are. Through love you are

157

the best that you are, and I am the best that I am. Love allows me to accept you just the way you are. Love allows our relationship to be peaceful, tranquil and loving."

See in your mind's eye this relationship healing and being wonderful. See yourself being filled with love and exuding this love to everyone around you.

Whenever you are ready, open your eyes and come back to the room.

The next step is to practice what you have asked for by being loving and seeing love in your relationships, and by being fully present and understanding of everyone.

Write down a list of people you have problems dealing with and make it a point to do this meditation every day for two weeks.

- _____

- _____

Japa or Mantra Meditation

Mantra meditation is the silent repetition of a mantra, saying over and over again something that means something to you. This might take the form of a single word, a phrase, or a paragraph. In Islam the whole Koran is repeated out loud over and over again, taking the individual to a place of intense attunement with Allah.

This doesn't have to be hard. The word "one" will work, (Benson, 1975) or anything that will take your mind away from thinking for awhile. The words might be "prana" which means *life force* in Sanskrit or "chi" which means *life force* in Chinese. The words "OM" and "AH" have been around for thousands of years and are great words for mantra meditation.

You might even count from one to ten and then start over again. Words that mean something to you seem to work the best. Some like to use a prayer, such as the "Lord's Prayer," as a mantra. Still others might like to use a passage from *The Tao of Pooh*. Here is a sample:

> *To know the Way*
> > *We go the Way;*
> > *The way we do*
> > *The things we do.*
> > *It's all there in front of you,*
> > *But if you try too hard to see it,*
> > *You'll only become confused.*
>
> > *I am me,*
> > *And you are you,*
> > *As you can see;*
> > *But when you do*
> > *The things that you can do,*
> > *You will find the Way,*
> > *And the Way will follow you.*
> > > (Benjamin Hoff, 1982)

Some people use the words *"Om Namah Shivaya"* from Sanskrit that means *"I honor my inner Self"* (Siddha Yoga Meditation Center, 1993).

You can use a mantra while walking, jogging, running or doing daily activities that don't need your full attention.

Start out by getting comfortable, taking a couple of deep breaths and relaxing as you let go of all bodily tension. Then start the mantra, saying it over and over until it takes over your mind. If a nagging thought comes in, say to yourself "I see that, but not now," and go back to your mantra. Repeat the word, phrase or prayer you have decided to use, and again whenever a thought comes into your mind, say to yourself "I see that, but not now," and go back to the mantra.

Create your own mantra and use it to change your life.

- _____

- _____

Chanting

Chanting is another way of using a mantra to meditate. You might use the same words used in silent mantra meditation to chant out loud. Or you could find songs to chant such as old Chinese chants, or Sanskrit Indian chants, or Native American chants. Whatever it is, fully emerge yourself in the words, concentrating on letting the words take over your mind. If a thought does enter your mind, say to yourself silently "I see that, but not right now," and go back to concentrating on the chant.

Make up some word or use words that have great meaning to you and chant them. Write a chant for yourself below

.

• _____

• _____

Summary of Meditation

Take the time to spend thirty minutes a day in meditation, though even a minute will help. Think of all the time you spend in front of the television. Turn it off and be alone with yourself. Learn to enjoy your own company. You're the best friend you can have.

Someone once told me they had been meditating for years and had found nothing in the process of meditation. Well, *that's what it is all about*, doing nothing, being at peace with oneself, having inner calmness and being free of distractions. Meditation doesn't *do* anything, at least not that one can see from the outside. It is all on the inside. I feel it is kind of like faith—you can do nothing with it—but you can do nothing without it.

Write down a time for being quiet.

• _____

Is it hard finding time just to do nothing? Then you need to be quiet more than ever!

List six reasons it would be of benefit to sit quietly for 20 to 30 minutes each day.

1._____

2._____

3._____

4._____

5._____

6._____

Now you have to put together the time and discipline in order to have this time alone each day.

The Body

Here in this body are the sacred rivers:
Here are the sun and moon as well as
All the pilgrimage places…
I have not encountered another
Temple as blissful as my own body.

—Saraha

1. **Do you take time to exercise every day?**
2. **Do you eat right?**
3. **Are you committed to staying healthy?**
4. **Are you noticing changes in your body with which you are not happy?**
5. **Is it harder to do the things you used to do?**
6. **Do you have aches and pains on a regular basis?**

Take Time for Your Body

Your body is the vehicle for living life on this planet. You can decide either to take care of it in a pleasant manner or you can ignore it altogether. In the latter case your body will not respond when you need it.

You may find having to be contained in this form of flesh and bone very confining. But this form is the best you have to work with and will work even better if you take care of it.

Just like your car, if you don't take care of your body you won't be able to use it for your travels in life.

It doesn't take much to keep in shape. In fact, in Ayervedic Medicine (an ancient system of medicine from India based on keeping a person well instead of dealing with disease) it is said the only exercise needed is yoga and walking. Being a personal trainer, my viewpoint is that we need a little more than that, but everything makes a difference.

A sedentary lifestyle has been implicated in all kinds of problems including heart conditions, cancer, varicose veins, blood pooling in the extremities, loss of energy, obesity, high cholesterol levels, depression, and the list goes on.

The key to a long life is to keep moving and to eat properly. What you do is really not as important as the motion itself. Finding balance in all areas of your life will keep you happy and healthy.

I know people who walk regularly and are in great shape, and others who swim and feel wonderful. Find some activity you really love, perhaps gardening, biking, tennis, hiking, or dancing. Whatever it is, make sure there is some kind of motion to it.

Your body cannot be put off until tomorrow. It needs attention every day. Could you stop talking to your children for a year and then expect them to feel loving and close to you? Then how can you expect your body to feel wonderful when you ignore it?

Do you have children? Do you want them to take care of themselves? Be the role model they need, and get out and exercise. Children with parents who exercise also tend to exercise, so take time and show them how.

I know of a man 91 years old who would not exercise. He had terrible muscle tone and fell down frequently. His next step would be a wheelchair. Don't become like that—get up, get out, and get moving! I guarantee at the end of three months you will be hooked on exercise if you stick with it. Exercise is like any other discipline. If you stick with it long enough, sooner or later you will begin to enjoy it. It is hard at first, but consider this: that 91-year old man found getting out and walking very hard for him. But with effort, he began walking farther and farther as time went on. At first he could only walk a block before having to sit down. But now he is able to walk half a mile and soon it will be a mile and in the future I see him walking many miles.

The other day I noticed a woman in her 80's jogging, moving along the best she could...now that's moving forward in life!

Priorities

If you find yourself always having (letting?) things get in the way of having a balanced diet or exercising, you should look at your priorities. Are you a priority in your own life? If not, why not?

List the reasons you are not a priority in your own life.

- _____

- _____

- _____

What came up for you? Why are you important? Or did you find that you think you're not worthy of your own attention? Where did you learn that? Write it all down.

- _____

- _____

- _____

Consider that you are worthy of your own attention. You were born perfect and no matter what you do, you are a wonderful person just the way you are.

Now write down a list of reasons why you are worthy.

- _____

- _____

- _____

Look at this list every day and say to yourself, "I Love My Self" over and over again. It is time to start caring for *you.*

Nutrition

First of all you have to fuel the engine before you can get it moving. This means eating nutritious, well-balanced meals. Like a computer, if you put junk in you will get junk out. Our bodies work the same way. Eat nutritious meals and you will have the energy necessary to work out and rebuild your body and immune system.

Take The Time to Eat Right

Take the time to eat right. Make your lunch ahead of time, that way you will have a lunch instead of skipping lunch. Plus making your lunch ahead of time keeps you from rushing around in the morning trying to get everything done. Think about your body when you eat. Think about what fast food does to arteries. Eat nutritious meals, slow down and eat mindfully, and take the time to relax so you can digest what you have eaten.

Make a list of days and time and keep track of your eating habits. How long did it take for you to eat today? Try to lengthen the process out until you reach a time that is satisfying to you.

Monday ———————— **Length of time for meal**_____

Tuesday ———————— **Length of time for meal**_____

Wednesday ———— **Length of time for meal**_____

Thursday ———————— **Length of time for meal**_____

Friday ———————— **Length of time for meal**_____

Saturday ———————— **Length of time for meal**_____

Sunday———————— **Length of time for meal**_____

Breakfast is Important

Breakfast is the most important meal of the day. Take in most of your nutrition early in the day. Your metabolism actually peaks about seven to eight hours after eating. If you eat the bulk of your daily nutrition late in the day, let's say 7:00 p.m., your digestion will peak at two or three in the morning. That is when your metabolism is at its lowest and all those calories end up changing right into fat. It is very important to eat a nutritious breakfast so you can burn off what you eat during the day.

What Happened To Lunch?

Whatever happened to lunch breaks for Americans? Most of us are running around like crazy on our lunch breaks trying to get things accomplished instead of sitting down to good food and enjoying a leisurely meal. We are frequently eating on the run or not eating at all. This is not balanced living. We *need* to have a lunch hour.

If you go to Europe you will find people taking two-hour lunch breaks. People sit in a sidewalk cafe' sipping wine and enjoying a wonderful meal. Two hours later they go back to work and stay a little later in the day. They take time to just *be*, to unwind, digest their food, and let go of stress. What happened to us? We all need to have time to let go of stress and feel like we can unwind.

Prepare your meals ahead of time. Place them in microwaveable containers and freeze them so you can take them to work. This makes life so much easier in the mornings, and all of life flows better when you start out with the right feeling. Frozen food is not as good as fresh food but it is much better than not eating at all.

What is Balanced Nutrition?

First of all, I don't believe in diets because they never work. What is needed is a lifestyle change.

Good nutrition is balancing fats, proteins and carbohydrates. I recommend one part fat, two parts protein, and three parts carbohydrates.

Fats should be in the form of mono-unsaturated fats such as olive oil and canola oil. Stay away from any hard fat such as butter, margarine, shortening and lard. Hard fats clog your arteries and lead to heart disease. Fish oils such as the Omega Three oils are good in small amounts. Capsules taken once a day or meals of cold water fish three to five times a week are great. Red meat has a lot of hard fat in it so it is best to stay away from red meat.

Fat is in everything we eat from breads to candy, so try to stay away from fats for the most part. Use oil sparingly but at the same time don't be afraid to use it. We need some fat to metabolize and utilize fat-soluble vitamins. Fats are not the enemy. They are just something we want to decrease, so use healthy fats whenever possible. If there is a fat-free alternative, try it and see if you like it.

Processed Foods

Stay away from processed foods. They have so many additives in them they are a toxic wasteland for the body. All those chemicals wreak havoc on your immune system, endocrine, and nervous systems by causing abnormalities such as mood swings. We were never meant to eat and metabolize chemicals.

A study was conducted in which rats were fed Societies Average Diet (SAD), which included pizza, ice cream and steak. This diet was ground up and fed to the rats with rations of water and alcohol readily available. A healthy diet of whole grains, protein and vegetables was fed to another group of rats with alcohol and water readily available. The results were astonishing. The rats fed the SAD diet drank nothing but alcohol and the rats on the healthy diet drank nothing but water.

The SAD diet rats quarreled and were lazy, did not procreate, and had a shortened life span. The healthy diet rats lived healthy, happy, long lives, getting along well and breeding to increase their numbers. (Willis, 1988).

What to Eat?

Eat well-rounded meals of living food, lots of vegetables, fruits and high quality protein. Eat live foods rather than canned, overly cooked, processed, and dried foods. Many nutrients are depleted from cooked and processed foods.

Eat raw fruits and vegetables as much as possible. Eat the bulk of your carbohydrates in the form of fresh vegetables and fruits, using whole grain breads and whole grain pastas and other foods to complement your meal.

Eat slowly over a period of an hour and never gulp your food down. Chew your food thoroughly in order to release the most nutrients.

Eat high quality protein in the form of soybean products like tofu and tempeh, fish, chicken, seafood, non-fat dairy products, low-fat peanut butter, turkey, and eliminate red meat as much as possible from your diet.

Use mono-saturated oils when you cook, and use them sparingly. Oils such as olive oil and canola are the best.

Sample Menu

Following is a sample menu recommended for active people. If you have a sedentary lifestyle you will want to reduce it from five meals a day to three meals a day. Active people have higher metabolism rates and need more food.

The most important aspect is to gauge what kind of activity you are going to be doing in the next three hours and eat accordingly.

If you are going to be up and around and working out, eat accordingly—for that next meal in three hours. If not, cut back to accommodate your activity level.

Meal one—6 AM

Two or three hard-boiled eggs (minus the yolks)
Fresh fruit
One piece of whole wheat or rye toast or 1/2 cup of whole grain cereal and skim milk.
Decaffeinated coffee/tea, or water

Activity before this meal might be 30 minutes of running, walking, biking, swimming, weight lifting.

Meal two—9 AM

One apple, peach, banana or other fruit

Small can of tuna (water packed) with onions, celery, olives, etc.

One slice whole grain bread

One tablespoon of low-fat mayonnaise

Decaffeinated coffee/tea, water or diet soda

Activity before this meal might be 15 minutes of yoga

Meal three—Noon

_ cup of whole-wheat pasta salad with greens and 1/8 cup of non-fat mozzarella cheese

Decaffeinated coffee/tea, water or diet soda

Activity before this meal might be 20 minute brisk walk.

Meal four—Three PM

1 cup of raw vegetables with 1/2 cup of non-fat cottage cheese

Fruit of choice

Decaffeinated coffee/tea, water or diet soda,

Activity before this meal might be 15 minutes of sit ups, pushups, pullups, squats

Meal five—6 PM

> 2 – 4 oz. Fish or chicken breast (broiled or grilled) with seasoning
>
> Small mixed green salad with teaspoon of non-fat salad dressing
>
> Small baked potato with a tablespoon of non-fat sour cream
>
> Decaffeinated coffee/tea, water or diet soda
>
> Activity before this meal might be 30 minutes of running, jogging, walking, biking, swimming

Note: Sodas and coffee are diuretics so for each 8 oz. of either of these, you will need to add 8 oz. of water.

List what you eat on an average day.

Breakfast_____

Lunch_____

Dinner_____

Snacks_____

Now list some foods you need to eliminate from your diet.

- _____

- _____

- _____

It takes discipline to eliminate unhealthy foods from your diet, but you can do it!

Close your eyes and see yourself with the body you want to have. Do this on a regular basis, many times a day. Now you have a reason for changing your eating habits.

Spice it Up!

Don't let food bore you, spice it up! Buy a few cookbooks and become familiar with all kinds of different spices. Spices add flavor and zip to food and make your mouth explode with all kinds of wonderful sensations. Spices like garlic also help lower your cholesterol and keep you healthy. Don't be afraid to take a cooking class. It is all kinds of fun, especially once you learn how to cook with spices.

Supplements

Our foods are totally depleted of most natural vitamins and minerals. In fact, they have been depleted since the early 1950's. I worked in a chemistry laboratory working closely with a toxicology department. We did many studies on pasture and farmland trace minerals and most of these tests showed that these soils were totally depleted of zinc and selenium. It is important to supplement your diet to make up for this fact. I recommend taking a colloidal mixture of trace minerals and vitamin supplements that provide many times the recommended dietary allowance. Remember not to overdo it, check with your pharmacist or doctor to design a supplementation regimen you can trust.

I personally recommend increases in the following supplements:

Selenium

Zinc

Chromium

Magnesium

Vitamin B-50 Complex

Omega Three Oils

Vitamin E

Vitamin C

Calcium (especially for women)

Herbs

Herbs are wonderful supplements and can make all the difference in the world in how you feel. Many pharmaceutical drugs are made from plants and are much more beneficial in the raw form than in the processed form. Herbs are drugs much like any other type of prescription you would get from your doctor. I highly recommend finding a competent herbalist who can help you pick the correct herbs for your situation.

Avoid asking advice about herbs from people behind the counter at health food stores. Most of them are not formally educated about the interactions of different types of herbs and such advice could be dangerous. Make sure you ask someone who has a background in herbology, such as a certified acupuncturist who is an herbalist or a certified herbalist.

Fluids

Drink lots of fresh clean water! Our body is mostly water and we need to replenish our fluids on a regular basis. If you feel thirsty, you are overdue. You need to drink water long before that dry, thirsty feeling comes along. People who don't drink lots of water start feeling tired and don't have the energy to get through the day. Much of our tap water does not meet government standards for drinking water, so consider drinking bottled water.

Another water that is available is called "Living Water" or "PiMag Water," this water is available through one company (Nikken) in the United States and has wonderful healing qualities.

Exercise

I recommend a varied routine of exercise. The body is an amazing machine but it wasn't designed to produce repeated motions over and over again. Sooner or later just like any machine it will give out.

Always check with your doctor before starting any exercise program!
Consider trying weight training, tennis, swimming, calisthenics, racquetball, walking, yoga, tai chi, qi-qong, running, biking, skating, or aerobics. Whatever it is, make sure it keeps you moving.

I recommend exercising about one hour a day. For some people two hours may be necessary depending on their metabolism.

If you like to eat, exercise more. The more you exercise, the more you can eat. Moving large muscle groups like your legs will help you burn more calories.

Here is a list of calories burned during certain types of activities.

Light aerobics	200
Walking 2.5 mph	200
Gardening	215
Lawn Mowing	240
Light Calisthenics	272
Light Weight Training	270
Housecleaning	272
Walking 3.75 mph	290
Swimming .25 mph	340
Badminton	347
Med. Weight Training	442
Slow Jogging	476
Heavy Calisthenics	544
Heavy Aerobics	544
Heavy Weight Training	610
Medium Jogging	612

I recommend working out at a gym three times a week and doing something different the other four days. For example, work out at a gym on Monday, Wednesday, and Friday, then walk, jog, play tennis or handball or whatever else you like the other four days of the week.

Start Out Slowly

Don't overdo it the first few times you exercise. If you feel sore after exercising once or twice, this is a sure way to become discouraged about exercising again. Of course you may feel a little sore, but there should never be pain involved in exercise. Pain usually means you are doing too much and you should rest for a couple of days before trying it again.

Balance is what it is all about. Build body muscles and strengthen your heart with cardiovascular exercise. The rest of your body can benefit from weight training. Muscle burns the most calories, so by increasing your muscle, your calorie intake can also increase.

Stretching

I highly recommend stretching of any kind, especially yoga. Stretching helps keep you supple and flexible, and I can't think of a better way to stretch than with yoga. It is also a great way to relax. See the section on relaxation for particular yoga exercises.

Try taking a yoga class. It is fun and I guarantee you will find wonderful benefits from stretching. In fact I wish I had started yoga many years ago. I would be much more flexible than I am today if I had.

Here are a few simple stretches I recommend.

Always make sure you check with your doctor before starting any new stretching routine.

Out of Breath for the Last Time

Tell yourself, "this is the last time I will be out of breath. I am going to change my life!" All you have to do is add a small amount of discipline and faith, and you are ready to be the new you.

List six ways being in good physical condition would change your life.

1._____

2._____

3._____

4._____

5._____

6._____

Now list what you do during the week to keep fit.

•_____

•_____

•_____

You say you don't have time, but will you have time when your body no longer functions properly and gives out on you? No one has time so we have to *make* time. There must be something in your life you could eliminate so you have time for exercising.

Make a list of things you do during the day that are not absolutely necessary.

- _____

- _____

- _____

Cut one of these items out — now you have the time to take care of your body! I know people who get up at 4:30 a.m. to work out. This is the only time they have available so they make the extra effort because they know it is important. Could you get up an hour earlier each day to maintain your body? If you are a night person, you might want to work out on your way home before settling in for the evening.

Weight Training

As we get older we tend to lose muscle mass and tone. This is why we need to push iron to keep those muscles shapely and strong. In order to enhance muscle tone, complete several repetitions with lighter weights. If you want to build large muscles, push heavier weights and do fewer repetitions. Always use good form and work with a buddy if possible. It helps if you have someone who likes to work out at the same time you do.

The friendship and competition increase the efforts you will put into working out, so ask a friend to join you

Here are a few simple exercises I recommend to help you stay fit.

Remember: **always check with your doctor before starting any new exercise routine.**

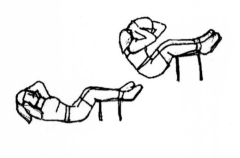 

Sample Exercise Schedule

Work out with weights or resistance machines no more than three times a week. Your body needs time to rebuild itself after having muscles pushed to their maximum on weight training days. Fill in the rest of your schedule with cardiovascular work such as stretching, yoga, aerobics, swimming, water aerobics, walking, etc. Keeping your workout varied makes it fun and exciting.

Monday	Weight Training
Tuesday	Cardiovascular Workout
Wednesday	Weight Training
Thursday	Yoga
Friday	Swimming
Saturday	Walking, Hiking
Sunday	Biking

Alternative Exercise Program

If you are one of those people who just hates to work out and think it is a real drag, you might consider what the Ayervedic Practitioners recommend. Ayerveda is an ancient system of medicine from India that keeps the body in balance at all times. Ayervedic Practitioners believe the only necessary forms of exercise are yoga and walking combined with a balanced diet, balanced lifestyle and positive thinking.

So if nothing else, get out and walk! Walk three to five miles a day and practice the ancient art of yoga.

Remember, as with any exercise program start out slow and gradually build up to where you want to be. It may take a year or two to have the body you want. ***Don't overdo it!*** If you do, you will end up hurting yourself and the end result will be that you won't go back to exercising.

Spirit

Come, Love! Sing on! Let me hear you sing this song—
Sing for joy and laugh, for I, the Creator, am truly subject
to all creatures.

—Mechtild of Magdeburg

1. **When was the last time your sides ached from laughing?**
2. **Can you remember the last time you acted crazy?**
3. **What are you devoted to?**
4. **What rituals do you have in your life?**
5. **Do you ever take time to do nothing?**
6. **Do you listen to your intuition?**

Part of Your Spirit is Your Personality

It is important to take into account what kind of personality you have. Your personality is part of your spirit. Are you a fixer, a doer, a controller, or a creative type personality?

Which of the following list best describes you?

A. Look forward to solving problems

Always have a question

Not very emotionalLike encouragement

Can be creative, yet able to get things done

B. Like to be in control

Need stability all the time

Hate change

See the problem and the steps needed to address the problem

Always speak up

Black and white on most issues

C. Like to take care of others

Enjoy your family

Peace lover at all times

Not into emotions

Love to be supported

Always too busy for yourself

Good at remembering things

D. Like to play

A Dreamer

Creative

Always learning

Like to help others

Romantic, visionary

Into change

If you pick A-you're a Fixer, B-a Controller, C-a Doer, and D-a Creative person. Of course you are a little bit of each, but on the average most people fall into one of these categories.

Take into account the type of personality you have. Work with your personality to make your life work. It doesn't mean who we are is either good or bad, it is just who we are. Every personality type is here for a reason. Your personality is a wonderful gift so use it to your advantage.

How might you use your personality type to your advantage?

- _____

- _____

Take Time for Your Spirit- Let Your Child Out

Child of Mine
Show me the way
Remind me of what I'm made

Frolic and tumble
Laugh and giggle
Show me how it makes me tickle

Remind me of where I need to be
how to get back...
that little boy I used to be

—-Paul Haider, ©, 2000

Take time to allow your spirit to grow. Take time off. Let yourself enjoy life. Did you know the average child laughs about 40 times a day? How many times did you laugh today? Life is not a series of problems that have to be solved on an ongoing basis. We must have time to wake up our spirit, laugh, and enjoy life. You can have all the money, health, knowledge, relationships, and social life in the world, but if you're not happy, what's the point?

How many times did you laugh today?

- _____

Get out and play, go fishing, go bowling, garden, play tennis, make plans to have a wonderful life. Don't sit at home all the time. What good does it do? You can accomplish all kinds of business goals, but if you're not happy inside, it's all for naught.

What activity makes time pass so quickly you don't know where the time went? If you don't know, you need to find out. Make a list of places to explore and other exciting things to do in your life.

- _____

- _____

Creativity and Laughter

Did you know when you laugh you unleash a major amount of creativity? Look at an office of people who just sit around moping all the time. Then look at an office of people who have fun and break loose with laughter. You will see an amazing amount of creativity coming from the happy, laughing group. Businesses are starting to understand this and are trying to lighten up the workplace so creative people have the opportunity to be creative.

A test was done in a leading business company among a group of ad designers. One group just sat at a table thinking of new ideas for ad campaigns. The other group rented some funny movies and had a great time laughing and then started thinking of new advertising ideas. The group that laughed came up with four times the amount of ideas compared to the non-laughing group. So you see, laughter can make you much more creative.

Find Out What Makes You Laugh

Go out and find what makes you laugh. Make a habit of finding new jokes to tell and find funny anecdotes people like to hear. We all need to laugh, it releases tension and helps us heal.

Write down what makes you laugh.

- _____

- _____

- _____

Now it is time to make sure you incorporate some or all of these fun-makers into your life.

How could you incorporate the above items that make you laugh into your life?

- _____

- _____

- _____

Is there something special you need to do to make laughter an everyday part of your life? Perhaps you need to be around more people, join a club, or start a group that tells jokes.

Write down what it would take to incorporate laughter into your life.

- _____

- _____

- _____

Being Crazy

When was the last time you soaped up your hair and created funny looking hair designs in the mirror while bathing? I bet you used to do that as a child. What happened to the craziness, the spontaneity, the aliveness, and the laughter that used to happen when you were little?

Just because you're all grown up doesn't mean you have to be serious all the time. Heavens no! It would be terrible if we couldn't crack a joke or act crazy for just a little while.

Lighten Up!

This is a wonderful world and you only go around once. Just because you are the head of some big company doesn't mean you can't have fun. As the old saying goes, "When it's all said and done, you're not going to say I should have spent more time at the office." Heck no, you're going to say, "I wish I had let my hair down more and been myself."

Are you worried others won't accept you as you are? But if you can't be yourself, does it really matter if they accept you? Don't sell your soul for acceptance by others. People who walk to the beat of a different drummer are admired. Just be *you*, be your own person, have friends, and have a social life. Be true to who you are. Most of all, be true to who you want to be. Most of us are not who we want to be right now. We tend to put on a happy face and become what we think others want us to be. Only when we finally become enlightened do we truly find the meaning to happiness: being ourselves. No matter how crazy, weird, strange, nutty or different, whatever it is you want to do, you should do it! It doesn't matter what others think, it matters what *you* think.

So—what crazy thing have you been putting off doing because you thought it was childish or absurd or just plain nuts?

List a few crazy things you would like to do now and in the future.

- _____

- _____

- _____

- _____

These crazy, fun ideas are what get your heart beating, make you feel alive, and create excitement in your life. And there is the laughter and fun they create along the way. Being crazy is good for you. Break loose and be *you* for a change. If you want to run naked down the middle of the street, go for it! You might have to do that in a way that keeps you from being locked up, but that's all right. Modify your plans so you can do what you really want to do. Perhaps you have to do it in the middle of the night on a foggy night. It doesn't matter, just do it!

We Need Rituals in Our Lives

What rituals do you have in your life? Most of us don't take the time to have rituals in our life. We run here and there and don't take even a moment to smell the flowers.

My father was from an area of the Far East, India, before Pakistan and India became separate nations. After my father died I went to the village where he grew up. It was like flying through some sort of time warp. I left the United States with all its hustle and bustle, and ended up in a country where oxen are still used for agricultural muscle power. The one thing I really noticed that seemed to keep Pakistan together was the ritual of praying five times a day. It seemed that even though this country was not rich monetarily, it was rich spiritually.

We have lost our rituals in life. It is time we found rituals that help our spiritual development. Of course some of us go to church on Sundays, but for the most part many Americans stay at home and watch the game on Sunday. And that's about as much ritual as we have.

I have rituals in my life. I meditate every day, go to church on Sundays and find time for myself to be alone. It is important to have rituals to be able to connect with whatever we believe.

Rituals don't have to be of a religious nature. They can be anything important to you and will help you through the day. Some people put together altars in their house, little areas with pictures of loved ones, special artwork with heartfelt meaning, and poems that touch the soul. Putting all this together in a place where a person can kneel or sit and contemplate in quiet for just a few moments provides a type of retreat. Doing this every day keeps a person very centered, reminds them of where they have been, and lets them feel grateful for all they have in life.

What rituals do you have in life? If you don't have any rituals, what life rituals would you like to start?

- _____

- _____

- _____

Devotion

Are you devoted to anything in life? Do you have some special project that means a lot to you? Are you devoted to God or your country? What makes you tick? What causes you to keep getting up in the (every) morning? What driving force makes it all worth the effort of going through the pain of making life happen?

For many people it is their Higher Power, Life Force, The Universe, The Alpha and the Omega, God. For others, it is their work, their hobbies, their friends, their loved ones. No matter what, people need something to live for. We all need some driving force that keeps us moving, that says we can do it against all odds, that we are worth all the time and effort. What keeps you moving and wakes you up in the morning raring to go each day?

John Harvey (1998) talks about spiritual tension as being characterized by a lack of connection to the sacred, confusion about the purpose of life, and an absence of self-knowledge. Spiritual tension leads to feelings of alienation, isolation, and emptiness.

Now write down what motivates you, to what you are devoted, and what drives you to live a full life every day? If you can't think of anything, perhaps it is time to take time and find something that lights your fire, floats your boat, and gets you excited.

- _____

- _____

Faith

You know what you are devoted to, but in what do you have faith? Do you have faith in Science, God, People, The Universe, Fate, Numerology, Astrology, Positive Thinking? In what do you have faith?

There are times in life when we all need something bigger than ourselves in which to believe. Just believing in ourselves and nothing else makes it really difficult to hang on during the hard times.

Problems that are unsolvable are always going to happen. Life is full of all kinds of unforeseen, unimaginable hardships every day. Why they happen we don't know. But if we have faith in something bigger than ourselves we tend to make it through the hard times and succeed in life.

While working in my private practice, I have seen many people grapple with lots of devastating problems. The ones who survive these problems always seem to be the ones who have faith in something bigger, be it religious or not. Believing does make a difference, it gives us hope for the future. Without hope there is nothing. That is why in poor countries that have catastrophes, faith and hope are the only things that keep people moving forward in life.

In what do you have faith?

- _____

- _____

Intuition

We are intuitive on so many levels, but we are not taught by society and our parents to rely on our intuition

> When we consistently suppress and distrust our intuitive knowingness, looking instead for authority, validation, and approval from others, we give our personal power away. This leads to feelings of helplessness, emptiness, a sense of being a victim; eventually to anger and rage, and, if these feelings are also suppressed, to depression and deadness
>
> (Gawain, 1988).

Have you ever noticed something from the corner of your eye and thought it was something important you should question? But instead you think, "No way" and dismiss the whole incident, only to have it all come to pass sometime later? Almost everyone has at some time or another. Why is it we don't want to know that we are intuitive? In this society, if something has nothing to do with knowledge it is unacceptable. But the things we feel don't come from a place of knowledge, they come from our souls and are more important than knowledge.

Many people are intuitive in many different ways. Some are intuitive about people, some about situations, some about what will happen, and still others about people's feelings. Intuition sometimes grows out of protecting ourselves as a child. We learned to know when someone was angry and abusive. We learned to pick up on the very subtle signs others took for granted, but they kept us alive and well as a child. These are gifts should be used to our best advantage as adults.

Don't deprive the world of your gifts. You have been given gifts for a reason—to use them for the good of all.

We all have some kind of intuition that serves us. What is your intuition all about?

- _____

- _____

- _____

How could you use this intuition to help yourself and others?

- _____

- _____

- _____

Intuitive Knowingness

Do you know someone who was born with incredible knowledge of something they never studied? I know of a person who has a knack for repairing machinery. He could tear a machine apart and put it back together in no time, and then tell me all about how it works. Another person I know is a great writer. He can whip out a screenplay with what seems to be no effort. They are both incredibly gifted people. They didn't learn these skills in school, they just knew how to do them intuitively.

Albert Einstein was a pioneer in his field. No one taught him what was going on in the new field of physics. He used his own knowledge and intuitive knowingness to make the world a new and better place in which to live.

Almost all inventors have intuitive knowingness. They have an intuitive sense that something will work which motivates them to see a project through to fruition.

Believe in your intuitive knowingness. We are so inundated with knowledge that we are not listening to our built-in knowledge which we have had since birth. Believe in yourself and what you know within your own inner being.

It is ideas that drive this world now, not machinery, not communication, not money, but ideas. Ideas change the world, ideas move mountains, and ideas make life different. If not for ideas we would still be working with rocks and sticks. The most important point, though, is to believe in your ideas and make them come true. Making your ideas come true is the hard part, working to make your imagination a reality is the proof.

What intuitive knowingness do you have, what seems to come to you without even thinking about it?

- _____

- _____

- _____

How could you use this intuitive knowingness to help yourself and others?

- _____

- _____

- _____

Down Time

We all need down time, time to *be*, time to do nothing. This is time to regenerate and get ready for the next spurt of learning, growth or enlightenment. Do you ever "veg" out, such as just looking up at the clouds and seeing what shapes and animals you see going by?

When we get very busy and don't take a break, our minds start to wander and take a break for us. If we just take time to *be* during the day we can be more creative in the end.

Try to get up from that desk or get out of that car and go outside to enjoy a few minutes just doing nothing. It will rejuvenate your spirit.

Do you take time to do nothing?

- _____

Do you feel guilty doing nothing?

- _____

Where or from whom did you learn to feel guilty for doing nothing? Write the first thing that comes to your mind

- _____

- _____

- _____

Now that you understand from where that feeling comes, could you allow yourself to just "veg" out?

● _____

If not, what would it take for you to feel comfortable letting go and feeling at ease with nothing to do?

● _____

● _____

● _____

Meditation Is Not Just For The Mind

As has been mentioned before, meditation is a wonderful way to lift the spirit, to check in with the soul, to make time for our inner being, to slow us down and to make us aware we are more than just tools for a corporate ladder. Use your meditation to lift your spirits and carry you through your day.

Read Something Good For the Spirit

I find reading something wonderful for my spirit each morning helps me get through the day. Take the time to read a passage from a book you find inspiring. It might be poetry, a religious or a spiritual writing such as those by Tennyson, Emerson, Rumi, Gandhi, Louise Hay or whoever appeals to you. Take the time to read and it will make all the difference in the world for you.

What would you like to read tomorrow?

• _____

Quiet Strength

Have you ever noticed that the boisterous, noisy leaders we have had throughout time are lost forever to obscurity? The truly strong leaders have been leaders of quiet strength and people who don't have to make a scene to be noticed and loved. They are people who let their convictions and dedication show the world just how much they care and how strong they are.

Quiet strength comes from an inner depth that emanates from a higher source. People who dedicate their lives to a higher cause, to a spirit bigger than all of us have this kind of quiet strength. Yes! These people are Gandhi, Mandela, Martin Luther King, Jr., John F. Kennedy, Mother Teresa, Jesus, Buddha, Mohammed, Krishna, the list goes on and on.

All of these people and more made time for spiritual practice. They made time to center on what is important in life, to discover what life is all about, and to discover what they could do to make life happen. Are you ready to make your mark on the world? Then perhaps it is time to make time for rituals and spiritual practice in your life.

Relationships

Love is an infinite Sea whose skies are a bubble of foam.
Know that it is the waves of Love that turn the wheels of Heaven:
Without Love, nothing in the world would have life.

—Rumi

1. **Do you have a relationship in your life now?**
2. **Are you in love?**
3. **Do you take time for your relationships?**
4. **Are you able to forgive?**
5. **Are you able to let go of expectations?**
6. **Are you afraid of being hurt?**

Relationships are an inevitable part of being alive. Part of our job while we are on this planet is to have wonderful relationships. If we go through life totally alone, I feel we have missed out on a huge part of being alive. The process of living is a process of having relationships. The more we allow ourselves to be vulnerable to someone, the more compassion we can have for the rest of the world.

When people die, one of the regrets they have is not having more close relationships. If you really want to live a full life, relationships will be part of who you are.

It Takes Time To Have Relationships

It takes time to be in a relationship, no matter what kind it is. If you want a great relationship with your father, mother, grandchild, spouse, no matter who it is, you are going to have to put in the time in order to have one.

Relationships are a lot like trees. You plant them, water them, and feed them on a regular basis and sooner or later you have a fruitful crop of wonderful memories.

Are you satisfied with the relationships that you have?

- *Yes_____ No_____*

If you answered no, what would you like to change?

- _____

- _____

- _____

How much time do you spend with the people you love? Do you make your loved ones a priority or are they just somewhere on the periphery until you have spare time?

- _____

Are the loved ones in your life important to you?

- _____

If you were going to die in eight months, what would you want to do during that time?

- _____

- _____

- _____

If what you answered doesn't correlate with what you said about how important your loved ones are to you, you need to look at this issue.

Always Tell the Truth

How many times have you told a white lie? How many times have you told a lie to yourself and believed it? We all have, and this causes all kinds of problems. When we lie to our inner child, to our consciousness, ignoring reality, we are doing ourselves and everyone around us a disservice. People never know who you really are. When you are totally honest with people, they know who you are and you don't always have to cover your tracks. You also don't have to constantly remember what you told this person or that person. It becomes such a problem remembering what you said that eventually you get lost, and you finally say the wrong thing to the wrong person, and then you are caught. Always tell the truth and you won't have to worry about what lies are said.

Most of all, don't lie to yourself, this only keeps you from growing. That negative voice inside yourself is the biggest liar of all. Don't listen to it, stop all that chatter, it is nonsense, believe in yourself, and know that you were born perfect and you are perfect, and you don't have to lie to yourself in order to *be* perfect.

Now write down what would happen if you finally told the truth to everyone, including yourself.

- _____

- _____

Make a commitment to be truthful to everyone around you and to yourself, including your little voice inside.

I_____ (Your Name) will always be truthful to everyone, including myself. I will only listen to my inner voice when it is telling me the truth, otherwise I will tell it to go away and leave me alone.

Date _____

Respect

Before there can be love, there has to be mutual respect for one another. If we destroy the respect we have for our spouse, we destroy our love for him or her. It is one thing to love someone but another thing to *respect* and love them. Without mutual respect, love will never last. How can you love someone whom you don't think is a great person? In countries that have arranged marriages, there is an amazing amount of respect for one another. Through this genuine respect grows a love that bonds those couples together forever.

Respect listens and understands, never judges, and allows the other person to grow no matter what they want to do. Respect never puts another down, never belittles another, and never finds fault. It enables us to look for the good in others and to show them just how worthy they really are.

Twelve things that love never does.
1. Love never preaches.
2. Love never talks down to a loved one.
3. Love never orders a loved one around.
4. Love never belittles a loved one.
5. Love never intimidates a loved one.
6. Love never manipulates a loved one.
7. Love never intentionally hurts a loved one.
8. Love never tries to get even.
9. Love never has to win an argument.
10. Love never takes advantage of a loved one.
11. Love never needs anything from a loved one.
12. Love never stops loving no matter what.

Do you respect the loved ones in your life?

- _____

What do you need to do to show the ones you love just how much you respect them?

- _____

- _____

- _____

Love

Love is easy to do in this society. We are bombarded with all kinds of innuendoes about love and what love means. First of all, you cannot love *anyone* until you love yourself. How can you have compassion and caring for anyone else until you have love for yourself? It doesn't work. When you care about yourself you are actually caring about others. This means the other person in your life doesn't have to take care of you. It means you are a fully functional person and you can take care of yourself all by yourself, no matter what.

Without action, love is just another word. You can say you love someone all you want, but the proof is in your conduct. If you do things that are not loving from the point of view of the other person, that is not love.

Love is a muscle you have to flex every day in order to build it up to a point where it is strong and healthy.

How do you express your love for yourself?

- _____

- _____

How do you express your love for others?

- _____

- _____

Love is a cycle of giving and receiving on a constant basis. Love is given freely, but we only get love when we give love. How can we expect love in return if we don't give love freely? It won't happen.

What changes could be made in your approach to loving people?

- _____

- _____

- _____

Unconditional Love

Unconditional love is loving someone *just because*. Not for what that person can do for you, or what you expect in return, but merely because he/she is human and alive. There are no expectations, no hidden agendas, no controlling, no holding back, just being totally honest and loving. Love wants the other person to grow and be all they can be even if it means they will grow to the point of leaving you.

Are you ready to love unconditionally?

- _____Yes _____No

If not, what is holding you back?

- _____

- _____

Expectations

I had an experience in the past in which I was going to see a lady friend. We had been seeing each other for almost two years when she had moved away. I was asked to come with "No" expectations, but I found that very hard to do. She was just being herself and I was expecting something I had made up in my head, hoping there would still be a connection. I have to say my expectations got in the way of enjoying our visit.

210

When things didn't work out as I had envisioned I was hurt. It had nothing to do with her; it had everything to do with me. We put people in boxes and expect them to act a certain way, all the time hoping they will grow and become more of who they are. There is something wrong here. *Hoping they will grow and then expecting them to still be the person they were?* There is no way. I learned a lesson. I had to go through some pain to realize I was boxing in a person who I loved. If I love her there should be no expectations of her. She lives her life, I live mine, and if something happens in the mean time, all the better. If not... that's life! People have to be themselves, living the life they want to live, not being put upon by others' expectations. We all have expectations, though, of everyone and everything around us. It doesn't mean it is good or bad, it just is. Knowing we have expectations and realizing we can stem the hurt when someone doesn't fit the mold we made for them can make all the difference.

Walk around and look at everyone around you. How do you expect them to be in your daily life? When they don't fit the mold we throw them away, or get mad trying to make them wear the mask again. We have to realize that change is difficult, and we don't like change, we want every little thing to stay the same forever. Now that's a bunch of hogwash, nothing stays the same, nothing in this entire Universe ever stays the same. Everything is constantly changing, and so it is that we will change, and we have to learn that it is all for the best.

Write down expectations you have of others that get in the way of love.

- _____

- _____

- _____

- _____

Now write down how you will deal with expectations in the future.

- _____

- _____

Never Assume Anything

How many times have you assumed something? If you are like me you've done this many times, and it has gotten you into trouble in the past. Does anyone really know what you are thinking or feeling at any given time? Of course not! So why should you expect others to be able to know what you are thinking? That is crazy! Always ask questions and keep asking questions till you understand what the other person means by what they say, or until you understand what the other person is talking about.

Oh, I know what you're going to say, "He should just know what I'm feeling by the way I'm acting." Wrong! That doesn't work, people are too busy to check on all the little cues you are putting out to them. They have a hard enough time just checking in with themselves! Give it to them straight, don't play games, this accomplishes nothing, and in the end someone gets hurt. Like I said **"Never Assume Anything"** and you will be much happier with every aspect of your life.

Now write down a few times when taking something for granted got you into trouble.

- _____

- _____

Now write down what would happen if you always asked enough questions to clarify everything.

- _____

- _____

Listen But Don't Take It In

When other people take their bad days out on you, is it your fault? Of course not! They are having a bad day, and you were just there.

At other times people are trying to work out their own problems and because we just happen to be in the line of fire we get blasted. This has nothing to do with us, it has to do with the other person. We all live in our own little world, even you do, so don't take what others have to say to heart. Take everything with a huge grain of salt. If everyone in the world did this we wouldn't have all the problems we have now.

If someone says something mean to you, or you don't really agree with what someone said, just let it go, knowing that they live in their world and you live in yours. Don't take on what others want to dish out, you're only asking for trouble if you do.

Write down a few ways how not dealing with other people's "stuff" could save you a lot of trouble.

● _____

● _____

Compassion

Compassion is the end result of love for yourself, love for others, and love for humanity. Compassion is loving those you don't really like. Compassion is understanding, feeling what others feel, being sympathetic and caring. Compassionate people are the ones who try to heal the ills of the world. Compassion is trying to understand what others have been through. Without compassion there is no love, for love can only exist in the warm womb of compassion.

Two monks were washing their bowls in the river when they noticed a scorpion that was drowning. One monk scooped it up and set it on a rock. In the process he was stung. He went back to washing his bowl and again the scorpion fell in the river. The monk saved the scorpion and again was stung. The other monk asked him, "Friend, why do you continue to save the scorpion when you know its nature is to sting?"

"Because," the monk replied, "to save it is *my* nature."

Are you compassionate?

- _____

If not, what holds you back from loving other people?

- _____

- _____

Allowing Ourselves to Feel Pain and Love Again

We sometimes find ourselves so hurt from our last relationship that we don't let ourselves get involved again. This is the cycle of life, however. Just as in birth, joy follows pain. We can't escape pain, and even though most of us don't like it, it is going to happen no matter what. If we stop loving, the cycle stops and there is no more pain. But at the same time there is no more love.

There is an old saying, "Love like you've never been hurt." This is very good advice. You *will* be hurt. People are human, they change, they make mistakes. But if you ever want to love again, you are going to have to allow yourself to feel the pain. Cry, shout, scream, be sad, be angry. Let it out and the healing will begin.

Have you let your feelings out from your last relationship?

- _____

If not write down a few ways to express your feelings, so you may move forward in this area of your life.

- _____

- _____

- _____

Fear or Love

There are only two realities in this life, Love and Fear. Everything in life boils down to one or the other. Which would you rather follow, Love or Fear? If you do something because you feel you have to, it is Fear. If you do something because you want to, it is Love. You choose, because it is all up to you.

Warmth

Some of us project more warmth and concern than others. Those who have warmth give it to everyone. This warmth is like a mirror; most of the time it is projected back at the person who sends it out. Everyone needs warmth and everyone needs to be held. We need to be cared for. We all need to know we are loved for who we are, not for what we do.

If you are a person who has a hard time projecting warmth, how are you going to receive warmth? Warmth is a feeling, it is not a certain type of hug or a way of being. It is genuinely caring about others. It is the heartfelt hand on the shoulder of a friend who is down. It is the phone call out of the blue to a person you know could use a friend right now. It is being there when no one else will be. Warmth is conveyed in so many different ways.

Do you show warmth to those around you?

If you do, how do you show your warmth toward others? And if not, how might you start showing warmth towards those in your life?

- _____

- _____

- _____

- _____

- _____

Trust

Trust is a major component of love. Trust is the foundation for all the rest of the building blocks of love. A home without a proper foundation will sooner or later erode away with dry rot and termites. The same thing happens with relationships devoid of trust. Trust is the mortar that holds together all the work you have put into this wonderful piece of art call a relationship. Without a deep, undoubting knowingness that the other person will always do what is best for the two of you, there can be no relationship. This doesn't mean your other half won't make mistakes…they will.

Do you trust others?

- _____

If not what keeps you from trusting others?

- _____

- _____

- _____

Listening

Are you being honored? Are you being totally listened to by your other half? This is a very important point. If you ask a question and your spouse never understands you and thinks that what you are saying is an attack on them, you need to find a way to communicate more effectively.

Everyone sees life a little differently. No one is going to see eye to eye all the time. Your spouse doesn't have to agree with you, but you do have to listen and make them feel their ideas are important to you. If you say something and your other half jumps down your throat and you don't understand why, you are not listening deeply to each other and your past experiences are getting in the way.

Does your other half blow up when you ask a question?

- _____

Then you need to find someone who can facilitate your communication problems. Get professional help.

Forgiveness

We can never love until we have forgiven the past and let go of the hurts of yesterday. How can we trust if we haven't forgiven someone we had trusted who has hurt us? We can't! We have to let go of all that anger and those reasons to hold on to the past before we can truly move forward with another relationship, for love is a never-ending dance of loving and forgiving.

Who do you need to forgive?

- _____

- _____

- _____

What is it going to take for you to let go of that anger?
The anger you hold inside is only hurting you. You are the one who is alone in a crowd.

- _____

- _____

Imagine Yourself in Others, and Look at Them Differently

Try this exercise: Imagine yourself looking at a person with whom you are angry and would like to forgive. Now imagine a ghost-like image of yourself walking out of you and into the other person. You are melting right into their body and becoming one with them. Take the time to see through their eyes for just a little while. See what happened between the two of you and see it through their eyes this time. Feel what the other person is feeling, what they felt at the time this incident happened, what they felt afterwards and what they feel now. Feel the experiences they have been through in their life. Feel every single milestone in their life that makes up the core of this human being.

Now imagine your image walking out of their body and back into your body. Feel what your image felt while it was a part of the other person involved. Let go of resistance and feel deeply what is going on inside your mind, body and soul.

Are you still angry?

- _____

Love is a very convoluted and intertwined feeling. It is intertwined with compassion, warmth, caring, trust, anger, sadness, joy, passion and ecstasy.

No Hiding—Let Others In

You can sit in the corner and never let others into your life, but that doesn't accomplish anything. If you want to have a relationship, you need to open the door. You can live a life of quiet desperation or get out and make a difference.

Don't be afraid people are looking at you. Everyone is too busy looking at themselves to look at you. Just do your best and you will do great. No longer can you afford to be a wallflower. Get out and take a chance, people won't bite. If you want a relationship, you have to meet people. Join a club so you can meet people in a new and different setting.

What are you going to do to allow people into your life?

- _____

- _____

Who is Winning?

If you get in to a mindset that you have to be the winner of every argument, then your relationship is going to suffer. Remember that your relationship is a coalition of two people bringing together two souls to become not one but two people in union. Two people in union who believe that the union is much stronger than the sum total of the two parts alone. If you win, your spouse looses. So how is that a win for the relationship?

Relationships are not about winning. Relationships are about doing what is best for the relationship and never forgetting the fact that the relationship is of utmost importance.

Do you feel a need to have to win all the time in your arguments with your other half?

• _____

Would it be all right to look at arguments from a perspective of having the relationship win?

• _____

Now how are you going to react differently during your arguments in order for your relationship to win?

- _____

- _____

- _____

- _____

Social Aspects

"A friend is someone who knows the song in your heart and can sing it back to you when you have forgotten the words."

—unknown

1. **Do you schedule time for a social life?**
2. **Do you have close friends?**
3. **Are you active in your community?**
4. **Who listens when you are feeling down?**
5. **Are you too busy for friends?**
6. **Are you tired of being alone?**

Take Time for a Social Life

If you want to have friends and be social, you have to make a point of finding the time to do so. It doesn't happen by itself. It takes time and effort to get out and meet people and have lots of friends. Think of it as standing at a huge buffet with countless food choices right in front of you and your plate is empty. It is time to stop living your life just going to work, coming home, and "cocooning" so much that you are all alone.

Are you willing to put in time for a social life?

- _____Yes_____No

How much time per week are you willing to set aside?

• _____

You Have to Find Friends, They Won't Find You

How many friends will continue to keep calling you if you don't call them as well? On the average, most people sit around waiting for the telephone to ring and hoping that someone will think about them and give them a call.

Do you really think anyone is going to contact you if you don't contact them first? Of course not. We are all waiting and hoping we haven't been forgotten, but everyone has a very busy life and because of this we put connecting with other people last on our list. Then we wonder why we are so alone!

When was the last time you made an effort to contact people?

• _____

Would it be okay to contact friends on a weekly basis? Write down your answers.

• _____

• _____

• _____

Is it time to schedule getting together with friends in your appointment book?

Set aside thirty minutes every week to connect with friends by phone.

If you look at a 168-hour week and figure 56 hours for sleep and 40 hours for work, that leaves 72 hours. Six areas of life divided into 72 hours works out to be 12 hours per area of life. How many of us are willing to work 12 hours a week on making friends. Of course, 12 hours is just a relative number and the actual number is going to vary depending on who you are. But it does give you a good idea of how balanced your life is. How many of us put in even three hours working on our social life?

On the other hand if you find you spend a lot of your time on nothing more than your social life, the domino effect is going to occur and other areas of your life will begin to suffer.

This is not a strict way of looking at life's hours, of course. When something unexpected comes up, you have to be flexible in order to deal with work situations and home life. If you consistently find yourself not putting any energy and time into your social life or if your life is consumed by nothing other than social events, you really need to look closely at what is going on.

If you don't have a social life, be honest, and go within yourself to connect with your feelings about why you don't, and write your answer below.

- _____

- _____

- _____

- _____

If a friend of yours wrote you letter stating they really wanted more of a social life, how would you respond to them?

- _____

What could you do to change what you have just written and have a more well-rounded social life? Write your answer below.

- _____

- _____

- _____

- _____

Take what you have just written and go out and change your life!

Don't be a wallflower anymore. Emerge from your cocoon and start enjoying all the wonderful people there are to meet.

Let Friends in, We Need Confidants

Did you know the more close friends we confide in, the longer we live? That's right, the more confidants we have to tell our worries, trials, and tribulations to, the better we feel and the less stress we have in our lives.

Studies have been made showing that older people with lots of close friends live much longer than people without friends.

How many close friends do you have?

- *0-1_____2-3_____3-5_____5-10_____*

10-20_____20 or more_____

Look at the number of friends you checked—do you like what you see?

If not, it is time to get out and start finding friends! But you say, "How do I do that?"

Be a Mentor

There are so many children and adults who need guidance: be a mentor! Put yourself out there and make a difference. Give some of your time. If every one of us put just two hours a week into helping others, this country would be a totally different place. We would not have half the problems we have now.

Children need mentors, and so do adults. For instance, I have six mentors in my life. These are people to whom I can go to for advice and direction when I'm not really sure what to do. We all need an additional point of view sometimes. We don't always have all the answers. I know I like to bounce ideas off people whom I respect and honor.

Be a mentor for someone in the business community or for your local Chamber of Commerce. There is also SCORE, a group of people made up of retired executives and business people who volunteer their time and help people who are starting new businesses. This is just one of many choices of organizations.

Children need all the mentoring they can get. If you like working with kids, look on-line on the World Wide Web. You will find all kinds of volunteer organizations in your area. You could make all the difference in the world to a child who needs someone to talk to and to share their time.

I know of a man who does just that. He helps kids find their way in life when they are having a hard time. He helps them find medical, psychological and financial assistance through the system. He does this because he cares, and for no other reason.

Write down a list of places where you might be able to mentor.

- _____

- _____

- _____

What is keeping you from helping someone else? Is it time, money, health, or that it seems like too much to do?

Then write down ten positive reasons for being a mentor.

- _____

- _____

- _____

- _____

- _____

- _____

- _____

- _____

- _____

- _____

Now how do you feel about being a mentor? It is amazing how a little positive reinforcement can change the way we look at any particular area of life.

On your game plan write down specific dates for joining a mentorship program in your area.

- _____

- _____

Give Back to the Community

Take the time to improve your community by joining your local Chamber of Commerce. Meet people in the local business community and start volunteering for city committees. Every time you go to a city planning meeting or an art commission meeting, you will be helping out your community and meeting new people who will open your world to a more expanded way of thinking.

Step out of your comfort zone! That warm cocoon of yours is very inviting, and stepping out of the cocoon is difficult. Doing something different from what you are used to will take effort and courage.

Make a list of organizations you could join to improve your community.

- _____

- _____

- _____

What You Give—You Receive

Whatever you give, you get back one hundred fold. I firmly believe what goes around, comes around. If you never give anything to anyone, you will never be given anything in life. The most important thing you can give is your time. If you really think about it, our time is the most valuable thing we have.

The wonderful man who mentors gang teenagers told me what he gets back from his efforts is a wonderful sense of satisfaction. "If I can make a difference in the life of just one person, it is all worth it." How many of us can look in the mirror and say that to ourselves? Not many! You can't buy fulfillment and satisfaction like that in a store. Being truly loved by your community, and seen as a wonderful person who loves to help others is priceless.

List below what you would receive as a result of giving to your community.

- _____

- _____

It is amazing what happens to your self-esteem when you start to help others. Stepping out of yourself for just a little while and taking the time to help someone less fortunate can change your life.

Join a Club

How many times have you said I'd like to join the chess club, or fly fishing club, or a car repair club? People in these clubs are all people just like you who have similar interests. They are all potential new friends. Oh I know what you're going to say, "I'm too busy, I can't join a club," then you're going to keep getting what you've been getting ...Nothing. If you want a social life you have to make time for it and clubs are a perfect opportunity to meet great new people.

Make a list of interests that you have and then find a corresponding club.

- _____

- _____

- _____

- _____

Positive Influence

Make sure the people in your life are a positive influence. If you keep falling back into the same group of people with negative traits and habits, you are going to fall back into your old ways of handling life.

If people in your life are not helping, they are hindering. You know who they are. It is time to cut some people out of your life. Successful people choose who they want in their life, now it is time for you to choose. This is not easy, it will be one of the hardest things you'll ever do.

List some people you need to eliminate from your life so you can move forward and be successful.

- _____

- _____

- _____

Want to be Loved and Have Lots of Friends?

Have you ever noticed that people who are giving have lots of friends? Well that is not a coincidence. Everyone wants to be around people who have a positive outlook on life.

I have had many of my clients notice that once they begin changing their attitude and become a positive influence in the world, people just seem to gravitate to them.

Just as Mother Theresa was loved for all her love and giving to others. So too can you be loved for the love that you give to others. Take the time to do something kind, loving and caring for someone every day of the week. If we were all to do such things, this world would be such a different place. You help others without expectation; but in the process of giving to others you will find that wonderful memorable events will occur in your life. Make a commitment to yourself to make a difference in the world.

I _____

on the _____ day of _____
make a solemn oath to perform one act of kindness every day of the year. In this way I am doing my part to change the world to a better place for everyone.

Compliment People

Most people in this country have low self-esteem and when a person is complimented for doing something their feelings of self-worth go up. Just notice how you feel when someone give you a compliment.

You feel good. It doesn't take a rocket scientist to figure out that people love to have people around them that make them feel good.

So give lots of sincere compliments and you will have lots of friends. Make sure you are sincere, people can tell when you are just saying something to give a compliment.

Financial

I used to say, "I sure hope things will change."
Then I learned
that the only way things are going to change for me is when
I change.

—*Jim Rohn*

1. **Are you working harder and making less?**
2. **Are you doing what you love to do?**
3. **Are you a workaholic?**
4. **What is your passion?**
5. **How are you helping others?**
6. **Are you using your talents?**

Everyone needs to make money to survive in this day and age. Of course, you say, and you have to work all the time in order to just eke out a living. But if you look at people who are very successful, they all work at jobs they love. That is the key; *they work at jobs they love to do.* When you are on vacation and doing something enjoyable, do you complain or get upset that you have to do it? Of course not, that is all part of loving every moment you are alive. This may mean giving something up in order to have something later in life, it is all a trade off.

Delayed Gratification

Delayed gratification is very important. If you need to have someone pat you on the back for every little thing you do, or you need to have an end result or make that purchase *right now*, it may be time to figure out what is driving these never-ending needs.

I know for myself that delaying gratification was very hard because I didn't feel worthy of having anything great and wonderful in my life. Consequently I had to fill the void in trivial ways to make myself happy in the meantime. Perhaps you would like to return to school but something holds you back. Maybe an ice cream cone will make you feel better for a little while, but afterwards you find yourself back in the same place where you began.

A lot of these feelings have to do with parents who were not there to encourage you to do your best and to let you know that no matter what happens, you are loved. They didn't let you know that even if you failed, it's okay because you tried. That's only because your parents went through the same process you did; therefore the cycle is perpetuated.

You can break this cycle, although it takes hard work and you must trust that you are on the right course, no matter what others say.

Are you able to do what you need to do for future rewards?
_____ Yes _____ No

If "No" what keeps you from allowing yourself to work through this inability to wait? (For instance, I start to feel insecure and need attention right away).

- _____

- _____

Write a positive affirming thought about what you just wrote down. (I am calm at all times and I can wait until I have completely finished what I am doing to feel good about what I have accomplished).

- _____

- _____

Now go back and reread the part of this book about believing in yourself.

Take Time to Work, But Keep it in Perspective

Are you a workaholic, working all the time, and never having time for anyone, including yourself?

_____Yes_____No

If yes, why do you hide in your work? Be honest now, is it because you don't like to deal with people? Does the thought of having less makes you anxious, or do you consider yourself just like your parent with the "Type A" personality? Whatever the reason behind working all the time, key in on those feelings and write your answer below.

Always go with the first thought that comes into your head other than "I don't know."

- _____

- _____

- _____

- _____

Work is work, life is more than work, and work is only one-sixth of the pie of life. When you die what do you want them to say about you at your eulogy? "He was a hard worker." Is that all? Think about it. No one ever said on their deathbed that they wish they had gone to work more often. Go back and reread what is important in your life. If family is important in your life, you need to put more energy into having time with your family. If travel is important to you, you need to place the appropriate amount of energy into leisurely travels. If being creative is important, you need to put time and effort into being able to work on creative endeavors.

What areas of your life are suffering because you work all the time? List them below.

- _____

- _____

Now list the amount of time you are willing to put into each of these areas to make your life more in balance.

- _____

- _____

You are reading this book so you must want to balance your life.

Now it is time to make a written commitment to take the time for each of these areas of your life.

I (name)_____
commit to making time each week for (List areas to find balance)

_____

in order to balance my life.

Signature_____ Date_____

Now use this commitment to change your life!

The Happiest People Are Not Rich

People who have very little money are stressed and people who have lots of money are stressed. Even Lotto winners are put under all kinds of pressure and many times end up unhappy. It seems as if having some money, but not lots of money, is when most people are happy. I know that seems to go against our the logic which says that a little money makes us happy, so why wouldn't a lot of money make us happier? Well, with lots of money come lots of headaches as well. In the end people with average or a little above average incomes are the happiest.

Find What You Love To Do

Try different types of work to find what you really love to do. If this is a problem there are many books on finding your perfect occupation. Read a couple of these to determine your type of personality. Are you a people person, a doer, a helper, a planner, a controller? Where does your personality fit among the different types of occupations? Find out what makes you tick. Do you love interacting with people? Or do you really enjoy being by yourself most of the time? Is creativity very important to you? All these areas must be explored and looked at closely.

Buddha said, *"Your work is to discover your work and then with all your heart to give yourself to it."*

Read one or both of the following: Zen and the Art of Making a Living or I Could Do Anything If I Only Knew What It Was to find out who you are.

If You Knew You Could Not Fail

What would you do if you knew you could not fail no matter what? Most of us wander through life feeling no matter what we do that failure is just around the corner. But what if you could not fail? Failure in not a part of the vocabularly of people who have gone on to do what they really love to do in life. And if you think you are going to fail you speak to people differently, and people interact with you differently. Self-confidence is knowing you can't fail. Because even if your project does not work out…it's not a failure as long as you learned something from it.

What you think about everyday will come to materialize in your life. If you think you are going to fail, what do you think is going to happen? Are you going to be able to interest a prospective investor in your company if you think it is going to fail? Of course not! So why do you keep thinking that way? Think according to the outcome you want to see in life. See in your mind' eye your company thriving and growing. You can do no wrong and everything is going as planned. Now go out and talk to a prospective investor. Know that you can't loose and you will win.

What kind of mind set are you going to have before you start any kind of financial project?

• _____

Now write down on a separate piece of paper a vision of your project down to the last paper clip. See all the details in your mind as to how the company runs, and makes money, and interacts… everything.

What Would You Do If You Had All The Money In the World?

Let's say you win a million dollars in some sweepstakes or a rich uncle leaves you a fortune. What would you do? Sooner or later you're going to get bored just sitting around. You will want to make a difference in the world to feel fulfilled.

If you had all the money in the world what would you do?

• _____

• _____

What Would You Do If you Were Going To Die Soon?

Let's say you were diagnosed with an incurable disease and were going to die in eight months. What would you do with the time you have left? Go visit relatives, take a trip around the world?

List what you would like to do with the time remaining if you were going to die in eight months.

• _____

• _____

• _____

Now look at what you would do if you had all the money you would ever need and look at what you would do if you were going to die in eight months. Are they the same things? If what you wrote is important (if you were dying) is not what you would do if you had all the money in the world, this signifies a problem and you need to rethink how you are intreacting with life in general.

What Talents Are You Hiding From The World?

I once knew a person who was a great artist but never kept any of her paintings. She would say, "Oh that's not good enough," and throw the painting away. The Bible tells a story like this:

The Bible tells of three men who go to Jesus. One of them has five talents (i.e. dollars), another has four talents and the other has one talent. Jesus tells them to go out and use what they have inherited to make more wealth. So the man with five talents trades goods and ends up with ten talents. The man with four talents trades and ends up with eight talents. The man with one talent buries his money in the ground. Jesus tells the two men who used their talents that they will truly find great treasures at the gates of heaven. But to the man who buried his talents in the dirt he says, "You will lose everything and even more by hiding what you have been given."

I feel this is true of our God-given talents.

Find your talents, invest them, and you will surely prosper and be able to give back to God and your community. But if you hide what you have been given under the dirt of "it is not good enough," or "I'm not good enough," how will you ever be able to give back to the community or to your Creator?

What talents are you burying (or hiding) that need to be exposed to everyone around you so you might prosper? List them below.

- _____

- _____

Take Your Talents and Use Them To Help People

Take your talents and use them to help others. The only reason we are on this planet is to help others. No matter what you do, whether you are an artist who brings joy into the lives of others, a financial analyst helping people manage their money, or a builder of software, no matter what it is, it is all about helping others.

How can you help others with your talents?

- _____

Do What You Can Do Today by Letting Go of the Past and the Future

Do you constantly dwell on the future by worrying about what might be? Or do you live in the past thinking about what might have been? Let go of all of that by keeping yourself busy doing what you can do today to make life happen in the here-and-now.

If something needs to happen in the future do what you can do today, including planning, to make it happen. The past is over and done with, so let it go and work on today.

What can you do today to make life happen for you tomorrow?

- _____

- _____

Relax and Let the Universe Open Up

If you are doing what you can do right now, you are doing all you can. Don't sell yourself short. The only other thing you can do is have a little faith. Be positive about the outcome of what you are doing. If you are positive, positive things will come your way. If you are negative, negative things will come your way. People pick up on how you are feeling and you need to be as positive as possible to make life happen in a wonderful way. If you say to yourself "this will never work," what do you think is going to happen? Yes, It is like a self-fulfilling prophecy—it is not going to work. Make it happen and be positive about everything. Think about it another way. You are interviewing someone for a job and the applicant says, "Well, I don't know if I'm prepared and this might be the answer to your question, but I'm not sure." Then the next applicant says, "Yes, I'm prepared and have an answer to that question because I've researched it thoroughly and I can express my belief on that subject." Who would you pick for the job? Of course you would pick the person who was positive and had lots of self-esteem. It is a no-brainer, right? So get out there and be *positive* and go for it! *Make* your life happen!

Say to yourself, "I am doing all I can every day, and wonderful, new and exciting opportunities are coming my way."

Core Beliefs

"As I believe...I AM"

1. **Do you believe exactly as your mother and father?**
2. **Have you ever challenged what you believe in?**
3. **Are you living your life or someone else's because of your beliefs?**
4. **Are you ready to change what you need to change within yourself to have the life you want?**

Each and every one of us has core beliefs about life. We formulate these beliefs during our childhood, acting like sponges to absorb all that is around us. Most of all, we learn about everything that is unsaid and acknowledge it as reality in our home. Reality is different for each and every person on this planet. We all see things differently, we all see through different colored glasses, and because of that we notice different things in each of our lives.

Suppose you were at the movies where the projection screen was make up of three translucent screens, one in front of the other. Each screen has a different tint of color to it, all in primary colors, red, yellow and blue. As the movie is projected onto the screens, each screen loses the primary color making up the screen. If you look at the yellow screen all the yellow is gone, on the red screen all the red is gone, and on the blue screen all the blue is gone. But when viewed from a vantage point of seeing all three screens, one on top the other, everything looks normal. This is what happens in life; we look at life according to our own colored viewpoint. Consequently we have a whole different outlook on life depending upon what we have experienced, what emotional attachments we have formed, and what we enjoy in life. Because of this, we create beliefs about what life is about for ourselves. Since we view life from our own vantage point and don't see the big picture, we can't truly see the reality of the situation. We see only *our* truth and nothing else until we become enlightened and understand the reality of truth.

Some of your beliefs may not always be beneficial to your growth and well being. Because of this, you need to change your beliefs as you change your world. Every day you learn new and exciting things about who you are and what makes you tick. Some of these lessons are painful and make you go inside and reconsider your basis for your beliefs. At this point we are open and able to allow new and hopefully more beneficial beliefs to take root.

Cultivate Your Beliefs

You are in charge of your beliefs and you can change them at any time. Make time to take stock of what you believe about yourself, about others, and about the world and life itself. "Re-affirm any beliefs in which you have faith. They may include religious beliefs or philosophical concepts in which you put stock. Use any body of knowledge which you find comforting: re-explore it, lean on it, grow from it, enjoy it (Colgrove, Bloomfield, McWilliams, 1976)."

What Are Your Beliefs?

Make a list of what beliefs you have. Are you a positive person? Do you believe in love? What is life all about for you? What is your reason for living?

- _____

- _____

- _____

- _____

- _____

- _____

- _____

Velcro and Padding

Have you ever taken the time to look at your values? Do you believe like your parents because you truly believe as they do, or have you challenged yourself to find out what you believe? Many times we take on what others give us so we are not standing naked in the crowd. It is as though we have a body covered by Velcro and we have attached pieces of padding to keep us from feeling our own way through life, padding that belongs to someone else and has been passed along. With personal growth we take off parts of this padding and allow ourselves to stand naked without fear that others might see who we really are. Some of us never attempt to take off the padding and even add more padding as the years go by. We build ourselves into a world of other people's beliefs and ways of dealing with life, and padding keeps us from ever having to change. For the padded person, change is very scary. At this point some of us have a nervous breakdown because we don't know who we are, all we know are the pads we have accumulated over the years, and life is so unhappy. Check out what padding you are wearing, it could change your life.

List some of the padding that is keeping you from being yourself.

- _____

- _____

- _____

- _____

- _____

- _____

Now write down some areas you need to explore to find your own beliefs.

- _____

- _____

- _____

- _____

What False Beliefs Stop Your Success in Life?

You know what holds you back and keeps you from moving forward in life. What beliefs do you have that stop you from being successful? Are you afraid of success? Are you afraid of having money? Did you learn that money is the root of all evil? Are you ashamed of your body? Did you learn that the body is sinful? Did you learn from your parents not to trust anyone? Did you learn from life not to trust anyone? Are you rigid and unbending? Do you flit away your money because you have a hard time controlling your impulse to have fun? Are you afraid to let others know who you really are? Are you so angry that you drive people away? *You fill in the blank.*

- _____

- _____

- _____

Are you tired of living this way?

Perhaps It is Time To Change Your Attitude

If you are tired of living this way, you need to check in with yourself and make changes. The first change to make is to find someone who can facilitate your life change. This book is only the beginning.

Who Are You Going To See To Help You Change Your Life?

Yes, you read it right. We all need help now and then, and now its your turn. Who are you going to turn to in order to change your life? Oh sure, you can do it on your own and when it boils down to it you are the one who really has to do the work. But having someone knowledgeable in your corner rooting for you can make all the difference in the world.

I recommend seeing a therapist of some type. Perhaps a psychiatrist, psychologist, counselor, hypnotherapist, life coach, a trusted friend, a mentor. Whoever you choose, just make sure they have your best interests at heart and not their own. This process of finding your beliefs and changing your beliefs and dealing with them can be the most important part of your life. From this point on, your life will be based on how your beliefs change. Because this is so important you should only trust someone who really cares about you. Your relationship with that person should come from a place of love, such as the love of a friend, the unconditional love of a professional for his or her client, or whatever the case may be.

> *You are on a journey,*
> *a journey of change,*
> *change stirs up pain,*
> *and because you love yourself,*
> *you deserve all the good things in life.*

That's why you are going through this pain…**It's time to live life to its fullest.**

255

Description of the Cover

MIND   BODY

SPIRIT   RELATIONSHIPS

SOCIAL ASPECTS   FINANCIAL

CORE BELIEFS

    Each area of life represents a leaf on the tree of life. The trunk of the tree must be flexible in order to survive the winter and bear fruit in the spring. The winds of emotion can blow and rattle our leaves... but our beliefs keep us strong. Even if an area of life breaks away the core of who we are still stands tall. The tree of life grows ever taller by taking in the nutrients of CHANGE, TRUTH and FAITH each and every day.

I WISH YOU A LIFETIME OF LOVE AND HAPPINESS.

Happiness is a river that runs between the banks of sorrow and pleasure. Once in awhile we run aground on one shore or the other and end up ship wrecked on the isle of emotion. But usually we break free and make our way down the river once again... Happy Sailing.

Paul Haider

Natalie Bieser is a professional artist
who exhibits her paintings nationally and internationally,
with her work in public and private collections.

Her work centers mainly on the natural world of mountains, oceans
and botanicals, giving way to a very personal interpretation.

At this time the artist resides in Carmel, California,
painting the surrounding landscape with an emphasis on
Point Lobos State Reserve.

For information on the cover and other art work done by the artist,
please contact her via email at bieser@redshift.com

References

Bechtel, L., & Gillespie, P.R. (1986). Less Stress in 30 Days. New York: Peggy Roggenbuck Gillespie and Lynn Bechtel.

Benson, H. (1997). Timeless Healing.New York: Fireside.

Benson, H. (1975). The Relaxation Response. New York: Avon Books.

Colgrove, M., Bloomfield, H., McWilliams, P., (1976). How to Survive The Loss of a Love. New York: Bantam Books.

Cowley, G. (June 14,1999). Stress-Busters: What Works. Newsweek, 56-63.

Davis, M., Eshelman, E.R., McKay, M., (1995). The Relaxation & Stress and Reduction Workbook. Oakland: New Harbinger.

Gawain, S., (1988). Reflections in the Light. San Rafael: New World Library Oakland: New Harbinger.

Hall, P., (1999 January) The Effect of Meditation on the Academic Performance of African American College Students. Journal of Black Studies, 29, 408-415.

Haner, S.B. & Thompson, L.W. (1994). Effects of a Music Therapy. Strategy on Depressed Older Adults. The Journals of Gerontology, 49 (6), 265-269.

Hanh, T.N., (1987) Being Peace. Berkeley: Parallax Press.

Harvey, J.R., (1998) Total Relaxation. New York:
    Kodansha America.

Hatfield, F.C. (1993). Fitness: The Complete Guide.
    Santa Barbara:International Sports Sciences Association.

Hua, K., (1977). Meditations of the Masters. Ventura: Thor.

Kabat-Zinn, J., (Author). (1996). Mindfulness Meditation.
    [Audio Tape]. New York, Simon & Schuster.

Kimmel, D. (1974). Adulthood and Aging. New York:
    John Wiley & Sons.

Kornfield, J., (Author). (1996). The Inner Art of Meditation.
    [Video Tape]. Boulder, Co.Sounds True Catalog.

Leigon, R. (1999). New Balance Website. Classes,
    [On Line]. Available: 1999.

Maton, K.I. (1989). Community Settings as Buffers of Life
    Stress? Highly Supportive Churches, Mutual Help Groups,
    and Senior Centers. American Journal of Community
    Psychology, 17 (2), 203-232.

Palmer, R., Shrock, D., & Taylor, B. (1999).
    Effects of a Psychosocial Intervention On Survival Among
    Patients With Stage I Breast and Prostate Cancer: A Matched
    Case-Control Study. Alternative Therapies in Health and
    Medicine 5 (3), 49-55.

Powell, T. (1997). <u>Free Yourself from Harmful Stress.</u> London,
    Dorling Kindersley Limited.Prevention Magazine. (1997).
    <u>Three Totally True Stories: New Walking Paths Yield
    Much More Than Fitness.</u> Rodale Press Inc.

Sarno, J. (1991). <u>Healing Back Pain.</u> New York, NY:
    Warner Books.

Simpkins, C.A., & Annellen, Simpkins. (1996).
    <u>Principles of Meditation,</u> Boston: Charles Tuttle Company.

Siddha Yoga Foundation, (1993)
    <u>The Practice of Siddha Yoga Meditation</u>, New York:
    SYDA Foundation.

Time Life Books. (1997). <u>The Book of Calm.</u>
    Alexandria, VA: Author.

The Relaxation Company. (1994). <u>The Big Book of Relaxation.</u>
    Roslyn: Author.

Thurman, C. (2000, January) . The Breaking Point.
    <u>Coast Weekly,</u> 14-20.

Tracy, B. (Author) (1994). <u>The Psychology of Achievement.</u>
    [Audio Tape] New York, NY: Nightingale Conant
    Corporation.

Willis, E.L. (Author). (1988). <u>Turn Stress into Success.</u>
    [Audiotape].Carlsbad, CA: Penton Overseas, Inc.

Bibliography

Anderson, N. (1984). <u>Work With Passion.</u> New York:
   Carrol & Graf.

Austin, V. (1994). <u>Self Hypnosis.</u> San Francisco: Thorsons.

Benson, H. (1984). <u>Beyond The Relaxation Response.</u>
   New York: Times Life Books.

Bethards, B. (1976). <u>Way to Awareness.</u> Novato:
   Inner Light Foundation.

Boldt, L. (1991). <u>Zen and the Art of Making a Living</u>.
   New York: Penguin.

Borysenko, J. (Author) (1994). <u>The Power of the Mind to Heal.</u>
   (Audio) New York; Simon & Schuster.

Borysenko, J. (Author) (1995). <u>Meditations for Forgiveness.</u>
   (Audio) Carson: Hay House.

Chopra, D., (1989). <u>Quantum Healing, Exploring the Frontiers of
   Mind/Body Medicine.</u> New York: Bantam Press.

Hanh, T.N., (1991) <u>Peace in Every Step.</u> New York:
   Bantam Books.

Hanh, T.N., (1975) <u>The Miracle of Mindfulness.</u> Boston:
   Beacon Press.

Helmstetter, S., (1982). <u>What To Say When You Talk To Your Self.</u>
   NewYork: Pocket Books.

Hua, K., (1973). <u>Kung Fu Meditations.</u> Ventura: Thor
   .

Hyams, J., (1979). <u>Zen In The Martial Arts.</u> New York:
   St. Martin Press.

McGill, O. (1981). <u>Hypnotism & Meditation.</u> Glendale: Westwood Publishing.

Sher, B. (1994). <u>I Could Do Anything If I Only Knew What It Was</u>. New York: Delacorte Press.

The Nityananda Institute, (1996).
<u>Meditation; a Guided Practice for Everyday.</u> (Audio) Portland: Rudra Press.

The Sivanada Yoga Venanta Center. (1993).
Learn Yoga in a Weekend.TSYVC: Author.

Sheehan, E. (1995). <u>Self Hypnosis.</u> Rockport: Element Books.

**Learn More About
Balancing Life, and Relaxing Into Your Soul Through
Retreats, Seminars, Training Programs, and Therapy**

Relax Into Success programs are especially designed to provide you with the tools and techniques which will increase your awareness, increase your productivity, enhance your life satisfaction. They will also help you find life goals, improve your health, help you find rituals for your life, and learn how to effectively deal with stress so you can have peace of mind.

Relax Into Success offers retreats, seminars and off-site programs designed to help the individual or organization find purpose, relax, and succeed, while enjoying every moment of life.

Paul Haider - Health, Prosperity & Leadership Consultant - also offers individualized Stress Management programs that allow you to finally overcome stress. This program provides you with fun new ways of dealing with life, changing your perceptions of stress into fun and excitement for life, instilling new habits, balancing all aspects of your life, which clearly lead to health, wellbeing, and peace of mind.

For more information on retreats, seminars and trainings, call 1-866-368-8399, email us at **relax@paulhaider.com**, or write to:

**Relax Into Your Soul Press
P.O. Box 51646
Pacific Grove, CA 93950
You can also visit our Web site: http://www.paulhaider.com**

Relax Into your Soul Press
Books, Tapes, CD's, and Learning Programs

Relax Into Success, developed by Paul Haider - Health, Prosperity & Leadership Consultant -, provides simple, proven tools and techniques to help people manage and balance their lives in response to mental and emotional needs. This nononsense approach helps people to open the door to untapped vitality, vigor and happiness throughout their lives.

Explore and experience more of the *Relax Into Success* approach to life with books, music, audiotapes, and learning programs.

Relax Into Your Soul publishing and products can be used by individuals, groups, or organizations to learn and sustain skills to function on a higher level of personal and organizational development and vision.

For a list of our complete *Relax Into Your Soul* publishing product line or for more information, call **1-866-368-8399**, or visit our website at **www.paulhaider.com**

**If you are interested in being added to our daily
e-zine list of *Stress Management Thoughts*
sent out five days a week,
called "Stress Tip of the Day ",
please email us at relax@paulhaider.com**

Printed in the United States
19485LVS00003B/34-60